D!RTY® GERMAN

Everyday Slang from
"What's Up?" to "F*%# Off!"

DANIEL CHAFFEY
illustrated by **LINDSAY MACK**

D0375715

Ulysses Press

Published by:
Ulysses Press
P.O. Box 3440
Berkeley, CA 94703
www.ulyssespress.com

ISBN: 978-1-56975-673-7
Library of Congress Control Number: 2008904138

Printed in Canada by Webcom

10 9 8 7 6

Acquisitions editor: Nick Denton-Brown
Managing editor: Claire Chun
Copyeditor: Jennifer Privateer
Proofreader: Abigail Reser
Interior design and layout: what!design @ whatweb.com
Cover design: Double R Design
Back cover illustration: Lindsay Mack

Distributed by Publishers Group West

Sag deinem Hauptmann:

Vor Ihro Kaiserliche Majestät hab ich, wie immer schuldigen Respekt.

Er aber, sag's ihm, er kann mich im Arsch lecken!

—Götz von Berlichingen

TABLE OF CONTENTS

•••••Acknowledgments

Für ihre Hilfe und Inspiration möchte ich mich bei Drs. Jeffrey L. High, Nicholas Martin, Jutta Birmele, Walo Deuber und Wilm Pelters ganz herzlich bedanken. Ohne sie, wäre ich nie Germanist geworden. Ein warmes Dankeschön an die vielen Freunde, die mir ihren Rat, ihre Zeit, Hilfe und vor allem ihre Freundschaft geschenkt haben; H.H.H und Sabine Preuß, Stefan Harbers, Timm Sander und Heike Poppen, Lothar Grüning, Jens-Olaf Pampus, Matthias Kopf, Andrea Jablonski, Harald Friedl und Barbara Neuwirth, Erich von Kneip und Maren Wood, Christoph Döhne und Sandra Kretschmer. Thanks to the Chavez family for accepting my friends from faraway places into their home. Thanks to all the Chaffeys, and the Etzler family. Thanks to Jello, Tim, and my brother Kevin for encouraging my shitty sense of humor. To my parents for their love, support and for allowing me the freedom to choose my own path, I am eternally grateful. *Für ihre unendliche Unterstützung, Hilfe, Liebe und Geduld, für ihr Vertrauen und Lächeln danke ich dem Licht meiner dauernden Dunkelheit Melissa Etzler. Ohne sie, hätte ich es nie geschafft.*

USING THIS BOOK

If you don't know the difference between *Scheiße* and *Schuhcreme*, this book might be a rude awakening for you. I wrote it with the intermediate-level German speaker in mind, someone already familiar enough with the language to get by. Maybe you've got just enough *Deutsch* under your belt to read the menu at your local *Schnitzelhaus*, or, maybe you're so hard-core you've memorized Goethe's *Faust* and can sing all your favorite *Rammstein* lyrics until your vocal cords burst into flames. Regardless of your current ability, this book will push you to the next level when mixing it up in German so that you don't come off sounding like a total tourist.

The most important thing to know about using the information and phrases in this book is context. Knowing the difference between formal and informal settings and their required forms of communication is essential to getting by in German society. I can't emphasize this enough. This is a slang book, a dirty slang book. Using the tips, phrases, and just about any of the vocabulary within *Dirty German* in a formal setting is the social equivalent of crapping on someone's living room floor. Don't even think of using these phrases with people older than you, professionals (any government official, professor, cop, etc.), your friends' parents, or pretty much any stranger, unless you're ready to seriously offend someone.

That being said, feel free to throw out any of these gems when hanging out with your friends, your friends' friends, or any other degenerates you might know; it's sure to increase your street cred. This is, after all, a book on slang, filled with plenty of helpful phrases and info to help break down the language and cultural barrier and maybe even get you laid. If you're afraid that you might offend someone, exercise caution and slowly slip into conversations with terms you find appropriate.

You'll be happy to see that lengthy grammar explanations and conjugation tables are missing from this book (I don't want to bore the shit out of you with stuff you probably already know or don't want to review). There are, however, a few important grammar-related points that need to be addressed. All nouns in German have a gender that dictates their definite article (i.e. "the"). This gender plays a vitally important role in helping you understand what's going on in any given sentence. Since you must memorize the gender of a noun when you learn a new word, each noun's gender is labeled as follows:

> (m) for masculine nouns with the article *der*
> (f) for feminine nouns with the article *die*
> (n) for neutral nouns with the article *das*
> plural nouns are always labeled as (pl)

Another issue that's difficult to remember, even for advanced students, is when to use the right endings for possessive pronouns (my, your, etc.). Since the gender and case of the noun dictates how the possessive pronoun ends, I give you the ending options in parentheses whenever I use a phrase in which your possessive pronoun needs an ending appropriate to the noun you use. For example:

> **Slap my…!**
> *Schlag mein- (-e, -en)…!*

The above example covers your ass when telling someone to slap anything…regardless of whether it's a *der, die,* or *das* noun. But, you have to figure out which ending you will need to use on your own, cuz like I said, this isn't a grammar book.

Because an extensive pronunciation guide would be way too long to fit within the introduction to this book and would never cover all of the many little nuances within German, here's a short intro addressing some of the more common pronunciation mistakes that even advanced students of German often make:

C sounds like the "ts" in "shits" before an i, ä, y, or e*, and like the "k" in "kill" everywhere else^.

die City (the City)

^*der Clown* (the clown)

G sounds like the "g" in "gay"* unless it follows a vowel at the end of a sentence, in which case you pronounce it with a soft "ch" sound, like in "ich"^.

der Gammler (the slacker)

^*hungrig* (hungry)

J sounds like the "y" in "youth"*, never like the "j" in jackass, unless the word is of English origin like "jazz." Words taken from French like "journalist" have a French pronunciation of J like "zhuh."

die Jungs (the guys)

Q sounds like the "q" in "question"*. Like in English, it is always followed by a "u," which makes the Q sound like a "kv."

der Quatsch (bullshit)

S sounds like the "z" in "zipper"*.

saugen (to suck)

V sounds like either the "f" in "father"* or the "v" in "vagina"^.

der Vater (father)

^*die Vagina* (the vagina)

W sounds like the "v" in "vaseline"*.

der Wichser (the jerk-off)

X sounds like the "cks" in "sucks"* (words beginning with X are rare).

das Xylophon

Y sounds like the "oo" in "oops"*.

der Typ (the dude)

Z sounds like the "ts" "in cats"*.

zahlen (pay), *die Zicke* (the bitch)

Umlaut vowels

ä	like the "e" in "ten," only longer
ö	like the "i" in "stir"
ü	like the "ou" in "tour"

Some other tricky pronunciation issues

au	like "ow" in "cow"
ae	same pronunciation as "ä"; use this transcription for typing on non-German keyboards.
ah	like "a" in "car," but held a little longer
äu	like "oy" in "boy"
ei	like "i" in "wine"
eu	like "oy" in "boy"
eh	like "a" in "day"
ie	like "ee" in "beer"
ieh	also like "ee" in "beer," same as "ie"

oe	same as "ö"; use this transcription for typing on non-German keyboards.
oh	like the "oa" in "boat"
ue	same as "ü"; use this transcription for typing on non-German keyboards.
uh	like "oo" in "too"
ch (after a, o, and u)	like "ch" in Scottish "loch," spoken in the throat
ch (after i and e)	like "h" in "huge"
ch (at beginning of a word)	like "ch" in "chemicals" like the h in "huge" too
ck	like "ck" in "fucking"
ng	like "ng" in "ringing," never with a hard g like the "ng" in "finger"
ph	like "f" in "fuck"
sch	like "sh" in "shit"
sp (at beginning of a word)	like "shp" in "fish poop"
ss	like "ss" in "hiss," in contrast to "ß," which makes the preceding vowel shorter. "ss" is used in place of "ß" in URLs
st (at beginning of a word)	like "sht" in "ashtray"

Now take your *Dirty German* and get dirty!

CHAPTER 1

HOWDY GERMAN
HALLÖCHEN DEUTSCH

At first, Germans can come off as a little cold, standoffish, and intimidating. Don't take it personally. This distance is built into their language and their public lives, so they just need a little time to warm up to strangers. Think of them as New Yorkers without the brash attitude. For the beginner, knowing how to be polite and when to use *du* or *Sie* in the company of "Zee Germans" can be a little nerve-wracking. This chapter should help ease the tension and let you mix it up without sounding like a total tourist.

•••••Hello
Hallo

Just like hello in English, *hallo* is a generic greeting that can be used anytime with anyone, especially if you're speaking formally to someone, like a cop, whom you'd normally address with *Sie*. But if you really want to break through the ice with your new German friends, try chopping it up with some more laid-back greetings. It'll score you some serious points if you say:

Howdy!
Hallöchen!

Howdy-do!
Hallöchen mit Ö-chen!

Hey Hey Hey!
Halli-Hallo!

Hi
Hi (everywhere)

Moin/Moinsen (northern/northwest Germany)

Grüß Gott/Servus (southern Germany)

Servus (Austria)

Grüzi/Ciao (Switzerland)

·····Good Morning/ Afternoon/Evening
Guten Morgen/Tag/Abend

Germans are stereotypically punctual and precise...some might say anal. Each time of day has its own special greeting and a slangy way of using it.

G'morning, everybody!
Morgenz!

Good morning, sleepy head!
Morgen Mäuschen!
"Mornin', little mouse" and sounds super cute.

G'day!
'Tach!

Hi everyone!
Tag zusammen!

Good afternoon!
Mahlzeit!
Mahlzeit is literally "mealtime," but no one needs to be eating for
you to say it.

Evenin'.
'Nabend.

Have a good one! (evening, that is…)
Schönen Abend noch!

Nighty night!
Nachti Nacht!

·····Me myself and I!
Mich mir und ich!

There's only one word for "I" in German, but depending on
what you're doing, how you refer to yourself must reflect these
changes.

I was young and needed the money.
Ich war jung und brauchte das Geld.

I'm pierced all over!
Ich bin vollgepierct!

I'm laughing my ass off!
Ich lache mich zu Tode!
Literally, "to death"

I wanna get blotto!
Ich will mich besaufen!

I've been bustin' my ass in class!
Ich reiß mir den Arsch auf an der Uni!

·····Let's skip the formalities.
Lass uns duzen.

The difference between using formal and informal German all
depends on whom you're addressing. Generally, you should
address older people and people you deal with in professional
settings (cops, bosses, coworkers, anyone else you don't
know) with *Sie*. When talking to your friends, animals, people
younger than you, and family members (regardless of age), use
du. This distinction is so important to the Germans that there
are actually verbs for using *Sie (siezen)* and *du (duzen)*. You
can "*duzen*" fellow students (and coworkers once you both
agree on it), but you should "*Siezen*" teachers and bosses. It's
like a rite of passage to be offered the ever-sacred *du*. Here
are some possible scenarios:

EMPLOYEE TO BOSS:

**Mrs. Schmidt, we've been having sex for weeks now,
don't you think we should use du?**
*Frau Schmidt, wir haben seit Wochen Sex, sollten wir uns
jetzt nicht langsam mal **duzen**?*

COWORKERS:

**Mr. Preuss, we've worked together for years and our
families even go on vacation together. Shouldn't we
use "du"?**
*Herr Preuss, wir arbeiten seit Jahren zusammen und
fahren mit unseren Familien zusammen in den Urlaub.*
Sollten wir uns nicht duzen?

STUDENT TO TEACHER:

**OK, Mrs. Sander, but if I gotta screw you to get an A,
can't we at least use "du?"**
*Na also, Frau Sander, wenn ich mich in Ihrer Klasse
hochficken sollte, kann ich Sie nicht weiter siezen. **Duzen
wir uns einfach**?*

·····How's it going?
Wie geht's dir?

"Wie geht's dir?" is like an old Nirvana T-shirt: it's comfortable, but a bit dated and worn-out these days. Try one of these slangy versions instead. Just remember that Germans take questions like "what's up?" literally, so be prepared to hear more information than you need to know or be asked for more information than you might want to give.

What's up?
Wie geht's?

What's going on?
Was ist los?
Literally, "what's loose?" or "what's wrong?" It loses its negative sense when used in the context of "what's going on?"

Nuttin much!
Naja es geht!

How's it hangin'?
Wie geht's, wie steht's?
Literally "how's it standing?" Best used just with dudes.

Shitty, my girl just dumped me.
Beschissen, meine Alte hat mich stehen lassen.

Awesome! I got my test results! Negative!
Prima, ich habe die Testergebnisse! Negative!

·····Whattup?
Na?

For informal situations "Hi, how's it going?" can be too long. Friends will often greet each other with just *"Na?"* It carries the same meaning, but saves you ten letters.

Hey bro, whattup?
Na, Alter?
Alter literally means "old man," but is regularly used to mean "bro" or "dude."

Whattup, G?
Na, Alda?
Alter becomes *Alda* in punk, blue-collar, hip-hop and other German slang, especially in Hamburg. It's kind of like how "gangster" becomes "gangsta" in the U.S.

Hey sexy, whattup?
Na, Süße? (when addressing a girl)
Na, Süßer? (when addressing a guy)

Whattup, jackass? (serious or jokingly)
Na, du Penner?

Hey ladies, whattup?
Na, Mädels?

Hey dudes, whattup?
Na, Jungs?

·····Pleased to meet you!
Es freut mich dich kennen zu lernen!

The easiest way to get in with your new German peers is to find out about them and, especially, to let them know about you. Germans are really curious…and sometimes straight up nosey. In any case, take their interest in you as a good sign. As an American foreigner, you'll be an object of interest and have an excellent chance to make some new friends. So just dive in and start choppin' it up.

Nice to meet you!
'Freut mich!

Sorry, I didn't catch your name.
Deinen Namen habe ich nicht mitgekriegt.

Who are you exactly?
Wer bist'n du eigentlich?

My name's…
Ich bin…

How old did you say you were?
Wie alt bist du denn?

How old do you think I look?
Wie alt sehe ich denn aus?

I'm a friend of…
Ich bin ein Freund von… (if you're a guy)
Ich bin eine Freundin von… (if you're a girl)

I'm new here in Germany.
Ich bin neu hier in Deutschland.

Got anything to drink?
Gibt's was zu trinken?

Is it OK if I smoke?
Ist es ok, wenn ich hier rauche?

Got a light?
Hast du Feuer?

Do you work or are you still in college?
Arbeitest du oder studierst du noch?

What else do you do for fun?
Was machst du denn in deiner Freizeit?

Are all your friends this cool?
Sind alle deine Freundinnen so cool?

INTRODUCING YOURSELF)))
SICH VORSTELLEN

My name's Krissy.
Ich bin die Krissy.

I'm from Florida.
Ich komme aus Florida.

Yes, my suntan is real.
Ja, meine Bräune ist echt.

But my _ginormous tits_ were a birthday present.
*Aber meine **Mega-titten** waren ein Geburtstagsgeschenk.*

I'm Kevin.
Ich bin der Kevin.

I'm from Alaska.
Ich komme aus Alaska.

I wrestle polar bears for a living.
Ich bin Eisbärringkämpfer von Beruf.

I'm totally ripped and _hung like a stallion_.
*Ich bin ein echter Muskelpietsch und auch **ein Drei-beiner**.*

Are you from around here?
Kommst du denn hier aus der Gegend?

Do you mind showing me around the city?
Kannst du mir ein bisschen von der Stadt zeigen?

Can I give you my cell phone number?
Darf ich dir meine Handynummer geben?

·····Long time no see!
Lange nicht gesehen!

Catching up with old friends is just as important to Germans as it is for English speakers. Once the Germans have warmed up to you, they really let loose.

It's been a while!
Ist 'ne Weile her!

Where've ya been hiding?
Wo hast du dich versteckt?

Everything cool?
Alles paletti?

I've been way too busy!
Ich habe viel um die Ohren gehabt!

Lookin' good man!
Du siehst aber toll aus!

Man, you look like ass!
Du, siehst aus wie Arsch und Friedrich!

Whatcha been up to?
Was gibt's Neues?

Same shit different day!
Immer der gleiche Scheiß!

I'm stoked for you, man!
Alter, toll, dass es dir so gut geht!

•••••Please!
Bitte!

Bitte can mean both "please," "you're welcome," and even "excuse me," depending on how you use it. But friends aren't normally so polite around each other. They'll usually just use *doch* or *mal* to make demands of one another, the way friends in the U.S. do, as in: "Loan me a few bucks so I can buy a six-pack."

Pleeze!
Bötte! (silly and whiny form of *Bitte*)

> **Can you loan me five Euros, pleeze?**
> *Leih mir doch fünf Euro, **bötte**?*

Please please please!
Bitte bitte!

Pretty please?
Na Bittchen?
Literally, "little please"

You should hang out more!
***Du solltest doch** öfter abhängen!*

Gimme a call sometime!
Ruf mich doch an!

Could you grab me a beer?
Hol mir mal 'n Bier?

Just send me an email!
Schick mir doch mal 'ne Mail!

Chill out!
Chill doch!

Give it a shot!
Versuch's doch mal!

Do me a favor!
Tu mir doch einen Gefallen!

I hope we can hang out!
***Ich hoffe doch**, dass wir abhängen können!*

·····I'm sorry!
Es tut mir Leid!

Es tut mir Leid ("it does sorrow to me") is the standard way to absolve yourself of guilt in German. Depending on the situation, there are varying degrees to which you can express your sorry-ness. Among friends, there are even ways you can be a jerk about it and still cleanse yourself of wrongdoing.

Sorry!
'Tut mir Leid!

Hey man, I'm so sorry!
Mensch, tut mir echt Leid!

I'm fucking sorry!
Tut mir fucking Leid!

Sry (chats/texts/emails)
Srz

Sry, ur gonna be a daddy! (chats/texts/emails)
Srz, DUWIPA! (Sorry, Du wirst Papa!)

Don't panic!
Keine Panik!

·····Excuse me!
Entschuldigung!

As in English, "excuse me" in German can be used to get someone's attention or to apologize for a party foul. Germans have a bunch of slangy ways to apologize for mistakes and take responsibility for their fuckups.

'Scuse me!
'Tschuldigung!

Excuse...
Verzeih mir...

> **my broke-ass German.**
> *mein fieses Deutsch.*

> **my B.O.**
> *mein Körpergeruch.*

> **my bad breath.**
> *meinen Mundpups.*
> Literally, "fart-mouth"

Oopsy!
Oopsala!

'Scuse me for burping!
Rülpsala!

'Scuse me for farting!
Furzsala!

Pardon me?/Come again?
Wie bitte?

It's no big deal!
Mach dir nichts daraus!

It's only a scratch!
Ist ja nur ein Kratzer!

I'll buy you a new one!
Ich kauf dir doch ein Neues!

·····See you later!
Auf Wiedersehen

Auf Wiedersehen literally means "until we see each other again," and implies that you actually desire to do so. As specific as Germans are about speech and, well, just about everything, this implies that you hope to literally see them again. Sometimes you really don't, though, so you might want to master some of these phrases to avoid giving the wrong impression.

Later days!
Bis die Tage!

See ya round!
Man sieht sich!

Smell ya later!
Bis Spinäter! (frat-boyish)

See ya!
Tschüss!

See ya later alligator!
Tschüssikowski! (cutesy, but not feminine)

Bye-bye
By-Di-By

Safe drive home!

Kommt gut rein!

Literally, "get in there good," a smutty play on the harmless *Kommt gut Heim*—"get home safely." Best for when a couple is sneaking away to get it on, or you're wishing a buddy good luck on a date.

Ciao

Ciao (pronounced "tschau")

Talk to you later! (for phone calls)

Wiederhören!

Write ya later! (for emails)

Wiedermailen! (play on the Germanized *emailen*)

CHAPTER 2

FRIENDLY GERMAN
FREUNDLICHES DEUTSCH

•••••Friends
Freunde

Just because your recent German friends have started to "*duzen*" you doesn't mean that you're BFFs. As a foreigner you're a novelty, and most Germans will be interested in you and pretty outgoing because of it. But unlike your typical American, Germans see friendships as an investment. So it'll take awhile before they'll let you get tight like PB&J. There are varying degrees of friendship you'll progress through as you go from total stranger to *dicker Freund*.

Stranger
Fremde (m/f)

Some stranger walked up and smacked my ass!
*Ein **Fremder** kam mir zu und packte mich am Arsch!*

Acquaintance
Bekannte (m/f)

This **chick my sister knows** thinks you're the bomb!
*Eine **Bekannte von meiner Schwester** findet dich total geil!*

Fellow student
Mitstudent (m/f) (-in)

A **girl in Stefan's course** is banging the professor.
*Eine **Mitstudentin von Stefan** vögelt den Prof.*

Coworker
Arbeitskollege (m/f) (-in)

He's totally in love with his **coworker** Wolfgang.
*Er hat sich in seinen **Arbeitskollegen** Wolfgang verknallt.*

Chat-buddy
Chatfreund (m/f) (-in)

He's got no real friends, only a **chat-buddy**.
*Der hat zwar keine echten Freunde, nur einen **Chatfreund**.*

Pal/Buddy
Kumpel (m/f) (-in)

Matthias is a real **pal**, he'll do just about anything!
*Matthias ist ein echter **Kumpel**, der macht jeden Scheiß mit!*

Homie/Gangsta
Kollege (m/f) (-in)
A more "gangsta" version of Kumpel, usually used among hip-hop kids and immigrants like Turks and Turkish-Germans.

Watch it buddy! Ertan's **my homie**. Got it?
*Pass auf Digger! Ertan ist **Kollege**. Verstehst du?*

GiRLFRiEND OR JUST A FRiEND?)))
EINE FREUNDIN, ODER EINE FREUNDIN VON DIR?

The German word for friend, *Freund*, shows no distinction between boyfriend/girlfriend and "just a friend." You need to take possession of your guy or girl by referring to them as "my" (*mein*), or distance yourself by using "of mine" (*von mir*). Otherwise people might think you're fucking. Try these examples on for size.

A friend
ein Freund/eine Freundin von mir

Detlev's my friend.
*Detlev ist ein **Freund von mir**.*

No, we're not fucking, she's just a friend!
*Nee, wir ficken nicht, die ist nur 'ne **Freundin von mir**!*

Detlev is my boyfriend.
*Detlev ist **mein Freund**.*

Yeah, she was making out with my girlfriend!
*Ja, sie hat **meine Freundin** vollgeknutscht!*

Friend with benefits
der/die Fickfreund (-in)

No she's not really with him...he's just a friend with benefits.
*Die ist nicht wirklich mit ihm zusammen...er ist ihr **Fickfreund**.*

A no-bullshit kinda guy
ein bodenständiger Kerl

> **Lothar is the shit, man. A real no-bullshit kinda guy.**
> *Lothar ist der Hammer. **Ein echt bodenständiger Kerl**.*

Best friends
dicke Freunde
Literally, "thick friends"

> **Of course I loaned him my leather pants, we're best friends.**
> *Klar, habe ich ihm meine Lederhose geliehen, wir sind doch **dicke Freunde**.*

Partners in crime
Wie Pech und Schwefel
Literally, "like tar and sulfur"

> **We're stuck together like white on rice!**
> *Wir halten zusammen **wie Pech und Schwefel**!*

·····Chitchat
Quatschen

As much as Germans pride themselves on their deep intellectual conversations, they still love to hang out, have a beer, and toss around some mindless bullshit. Save the Nietzsche for your thesis advisor and keep it light and breezy as you ease into the crowd.

> **To bullshit/shoot the shit/chitchat**
> *quatschen*

> > **We just hung out and shot the shit.**
> > *Wir haben einfach **gequatscht**.*

> **Dude, where'd you get that jacket?**
> *Na, wo hast'e die geile Jacke her?*

> **My friends back home would love you guys!**
> *Meine Freunde zuhause würden euch lieben!*

> **So what's the deal with Oktoberfest anyway?**
> *Na also wirklich, was ist mit dem Oktoberfest?*

> **Do lots of German girls get tramp-stamps too?**
> *Haben viele deutsche Mädels auch **Tussistempel**?*

Wow, you look just like the singer from Tokio Hotel!
Wow, du siehst aus wie der Typ von Tokio Hotel!

Are all German girls beautiful, smart and funny? Or just you?
Sind alle deutsche Mädchen schön, lustig und intelligent? Oder nur du?

·····Family…
die Familie…

The modern German family can be just as normal or dysfunctional as its American cousin. Your new friends might have divorced parents, a trophy wife stepmom, two gay dads, or a creepy brother who lives in the basement huffing paint all day. But no matter how cool their families seem to you, your friends are likely to bitch about them. Also like in the States, regardless of how laid-back your friends might be with their own parental units, *you* still have to call them "Mr. and Mrs. So and So" and "*siezen*" them until offered otherwise.

Mrs.
Frau

> **Nice to meet you, Mrs. Sander.**
> *Es freut mich Sie kennen zu lernen, Frau Sander.*

Mr.
Herr

> **A pleasure to make your acquaintance, Mr. Sander.**
> *Mich freut es Ihre Bekanntschaft zu machen, Herr Sander.*

Mother
Mutter (f)

> **You remind me a lot of my mother.**
> *Sie erinnern mich an meine Mutter.*

Mom
Mama (f)

> **My mom**'s the nicest lady you'll ever meet.
> ***Meine Mama** ist die liebste Frau der Welt.*

My old lady
Meine Alte

> **My old lady** is a real bitch!
> ***Meine Alte** ist 'ne echte Ziege!*
> Literally, an "old goat"

Father
Vater (m)

> **My father** is a tax accountant and hates his career.
> ***Mein Vater** ist Steuerberater und hasst seine Karriere.*

Dad
Papa (m)

> **My dad** never calls on my birthday.
> ***Mein Papa** ruft mich nie zu meinem Geburtstag an.*

My old man
Mein Alter

> **My old man** is a real alki!
> ***Mein Alter** ist voll der Säufer!*

·····Personalities
Persönlichkeiten

The assortment of people you'll meet in Germany is as varied as the sausage selection at the local *Metzger*, and chances are that your new friends will have a slang term for each one.

Sweet
süß

> Ain't you just **the sweetest thing**?
> *Bist du nicht **süß**?*

really, um, nice
As in, "I can't think of anything good about this person so I'll call them 'really nice.'"
ganz nett

> **Dorothea is a, um, really nice girl.**
> *Dorothea ist ja **ganz nett**.*

Likeable
sympatisch

> **Jens is a real likeable guy.**
> *Der Jens ist ja wirklich ein sympatischer Typ.*

Antisocial
Asi (m) (short for Asozial)

> **Martin is totally antisocial.**
> *Martin ist echt der Asi.*

Outsider/Outcast
Schnitzelkind (n)
A kid who has to have meat tied around his neck so that a dog will play with him.

> **Ever since Otto barfed on my couch, he's a total outcast.**
> *Seit Otto auf mein Sofa gekotzt hat, ist er echt das **Schnitzelkind**.*

Dumb-ass
Kackspecht (f)
Literally, "shit woodpecker"

> **My boss is a real dumb-ass!**
> *Mein Chef ist ein echter **Kackspecht**!*

Jerk-off
Wichser (m)

> **Hey, watch out, jerk-off!**
> *Eh, du **Wichser**, pass auf!*

Smart-ass
Klugscheißer (m)
Literally, a "clever shitter"

> **He's always got something shitty to say, the smart-ass.**
> *Der hat immer was schlaues zu erzählen, der **Klugscheißer**.*

Loser
Loser (m)

> **No job, no money, no chicks, what a loser!**
> *Kein Job, keine Knete, keine Perle, was für ein **Loser**!*

Slacker
Gammler (m)

> **Since Klaus got fired he's a total slacker.**
> *Seitdem Klaus gefeuert wurde ist er voll der **Gammler**.*

Stoner
Kiffer (m)

> **Britta's new boyfriend is a total stoner!**
> *Brittas Neuer ist voll der **Kiffer**, eh!*

Mama's boy
Muttersöhnchen (n)

> **What, are you afraid, mama's boy?**
> *Watt denn **Müttersöhnchen**, haste' Schiss?*

Jock/Musclehead
Eiwoißtorsten (m)
Eiweiß means "protein"

> **You got no chance with her, bro, she's only into jocks.**
> *Mit ihr haste eh keine Chance, Alter, die steht nur auf **Eiweißtorsten**.*

••••Typically German
Typisch Deutsch

If you spend enough time people-watching in Germany, you'll start to notice how certain stock characters show up over and over again. Just like how in every American high school you're guaranteed to find jocks, rednecks, preppies, skater punks, stoners, and those super shy kids who turn out to be total sex-fiends in college. Here's a list of those people that are sure to pop up during your time in Germany. Memorize it so you don't get your ass kicked by confusing a *Hopper* with *Kanaken*.

Studis
Studis, short for "students," love to party. The German university system is free of charge, which means most *Studis* live off their parents or the government. Since they don't really need to work, they are free to party their asses off. Don't get me wrong, the average German student is dedicated to their education, but the open enrollment policy means that *Studis* go to class whenever they feel like it with little repercussion. This leaves them free to rage at the many beginning and end of semester parties (*Semesteranfangs/abschlussparty*), and hit up all the great bars and *Kneipen* that all German university towns have in spades.

> **Do you know where all the students hang out?**
> *Weißt du, wo die ganzen **Studis** herum hängen?*

Gruftis
Germany's answer to the Goth kids who used to eat lunch in lonely, pale twosomes at your high school.

Like their American counterpart, some in the *Grufti* spectrum are dark, sexy vampire/Suicide Girl types; but *Gruft* does mean "crypt," so the average *Grufti* looks like pale, warmed-over death. Their pasty complexions, dark eye makeup, black nail polish, knee-high boots, spiked leather trench coats, and long black hair (usually with some portion of it shaved to the skull) doesn't help either. Look past all that, though, and *Gruftis* will show you where the real nightlife is. Being nocturnal and all, they love to stay out all night and usually know where all the coolest clubs are. Just make sure they don't drag you to a Dark-Ages Metal show where bands dressed up like "Conan the Barbarian" play speed metal with twelfth-century instruments and Latin lyrics…spooky! Every summer the city of Leipzig hosts the *Wave-Gotik Treffen*, where twenty thousand Goths meet up to get drunk, listen to bands, and avoid getting a tan.

Germany has some hot-looking Goths!
*Es gibt total viele geilen **Gruftis** in Deutschland!*

Hopper

These blingin' kids represent German hip-hop. Believe it or not, not all *Hoppers* are "wiggers." They're usually a mix of ethnic Germans, Turks, Greeks, Africans, and anyone else under the sun. What makes them interesting is how they've adopted the best and worst of American hip-hop and tweaked it, Teuton-style. For instance, Germany has its own version of the East Coast/West Coast feud between Berlin and Hamburg. And although their fashion tends to follow American trends, you won't see many Grillz or Pimp Cups. Berlin's heavyweight battle-rapper Sido does wear a diamond encrusted silver skull mask, though. Now that's pimp!

I can't take German hip-hop kids seriously.
*Ich kann die deutschen **Hopper** nicht ernst nehmen.*

Schickimickis

Schickimicki is a sarcastic play on *schick*, the German word for "chic." It's mostly used as an insult to describe something or someone that's supposed to be classy, but is usually just pretentious and obnoxious, like wine bars and reality show stars. Like "pretentious prick," the term is usually reserved for guys who think they're the shit. You know, those douchebags who wear five-hundred-dollar sunglasses indoors, buy clothes that cost more than your car, and have a lifetime membership to the *Sonnenstudio* (tanning salon). He's a European metrosexual with the asshole mindset of the captain of the football team.

There are way too many pretentious pricks here.
*Hier gibt's echt zu viele **Schickimickis**.*

Tussis

Tussis are usually found in packs of three or in the company of a *Schickimicki* guy. Like her male counterpart, the *Tussi* is generally a caricature of herself: super tan (especially in the winter) and either very blonde or with jet-black dyed hair (nothing in between), cell phone-dependent, and expensively, but not tastefully, dressed. Sure, she might study business or marketing, but her real goal is to become a trophy wife. So she'll dump your ass as soon as someone richer comes along. If Paris Hilton were German, she'd definitely be a *Tussi*.

Martina is like a total Paris Hilton wannabe.
*Martina ist echt 'ne blöde **Tussi**.*

Kanaken

Originally used as an insult toward Turkish-Germans, the term *Kanake* is almost untranslatable, but has become a generic description for anyone who looks Turkish. Similar to how African-Americans took back the word "nigger," and gays took back "queer," *Kanaken* reclaimed the word for themselves. Similarly, you should avoid its use, unless you are one. It is also the closest thing German has for "gangsta," in that it refers to both people and a lifestyle. These "*Kanaken*" are kinda like small-time hoodlums. Your average *Kanake* hangs out with other *Kanaken* at bars or gaming halls in big cities like Kiel, Hamburg, and Berlin.

"Kanake" sounds kinda racist, doesn't it?
*"**Kanake**" klingt etwas rassistisch, oder?*

Penner

This is a mildly derogatory term for Germany's homeless people or *Obdachlose*. It's kinda like calling them bums. The term *Penner* literally means one who sleeps, only I've never really seen a *Penner* who was actually sleeping. They tend to hang out in front of train stations and market squares. They are generally harmless, unless they're drunk and start yelling at each other, which can lead to a fight.

> **I saw two bums yelling in front of the train station.**
> *Ich habe zwei brüllende **Penner** vor dem Bahnhof gesehen.*

Rocker

Rocker are a weird cross between greasers, party animals, and hard-core biker-gang types. A leather vest with an old "Ace of Spades" T-shirt underneath and a pair of lace-up-the-side leather pants and biker boots is their typical uniform. They will drink you under the table and then beat you over the head with it. They don't tend to mix with the general public, but if you do manage to befriend one of these guys, be sure to bring an extra liver because you're about to go on the bender of your sweet, young life.

> **Those rockabilly greasers stole my girlfriend!**
> *Die **Rocker** haben mir meine Freundin geklaut!*

Punker

More often than not, this is a squatter punk. Not to be confused with a *Penner*, your hard-core German *Punker* has many of the same attributes of a *Penner*. They can be smelly, dirty, and usually hang out with a smelly dirty dog in front of a train station begging for change; think Hollywood street kids or a squatter punk in a big city.

> **German punkers look tougher than the punks back home.**
> *Die deutschen **Punker** sehen echt härter aus als die Punker bei uns zuhause.*

Ökos

Your average German makes even hard-core American hippies look like seal-clubbing carnivores. In addition to introducing the world to Birkenstocks and communal nudism, the Germans are some of the world's best recyclers. The *Ökos*, however, take it to the extreme. Think of your worst "eco-freak" nightmare and then give them a degree in social pedagogy (kind of like a new-age, touchy-feely version of social work), and that's an *Öko*. *Ökos* are usually vegans, speak like they're talking to a five-year-old, drink Yogi Tea, wear purple socks, bathe infrequently, and seem like they're perpetually stoned even if they aren't. Try to avoid them…unless that's your thing, in which case you should be willing to shit in a bucket, chain yourself to a tree, or drink some homemade wine.

Eco-freaks kinda are a little too extreme for me.
*Die **Ökos** sind mir etwas zu extrem.*

Aktenkacker

Literally a "file shitter" or an "office bee" (*Bürobiene*), if it's a woman. German office workers aren't your average overworked salarymen. Sure they'll complain about only having six weeks of vacation a year, or how they had to work thirty-two hours last week and are totally worn out, but they are less hard-core than your over-the-top Japanese executive. Find them at an "After Work Party" (no shit…that's what happy hour is called) in any downtown bar. They're pretty easy to spot. She's wearing a skirt and blazer with a brightly colored blouse. He's rocking a suit with a typically German blue dress shirt and some weird designer glasses that you've never seen before. Chat them up if you wish, but remember: at the end of the night they're heading off together to screw and count their money.

These businessmen types have way too much money.
*Diese **Aktenkacker** haben echt zu viel Geld.*

Prolls

These guys are Germany's answer to rednecks, but they don't necessarily live in the sticks. In fact, they're more prominent in the industrial north. You can spot them easily by their mullet/hair cape (*Nackenmähne*), track suit, creepy molestache, and suped-up Opel Manta—Germany's answer to the Trans Am. "*Proll*" comes from "Proletariat" and the name fits. They're Germany's blue-collar best and for some reason they love parking lots. You can find them on the weekend hanging out at the local gas station showing off their cars and blasting *Böse Onkelz* tunes from their stereos. If you meet them in a beer tent at a local *Stadtfest*, watch out. They'll buy you round after round of *Lütt un' Lütt* (a beer and a shot) that'll fuck you up and have you singing *Volkslieder* until six in the morning.

Does every redneck drive an Opel Manta?
*Fährt jeder **Proll** ein Opel Manta?*

Omas und Opas

Grandmas and grandpas are everywhere in Germany, and German senior citizens are well looked after by the state and their families. *Omas* have a standard look: short and pleasantly plump with their hair up in a bun, and almost always wear a woolen coat and a fuzzy pastel beret. They usually have a little dog with them, especially on the bus where they'll give you dirty looks for listening to your headphones too loudly. *Opas* usually wear some type of sweater vest and the standard Grandpa hat, the *Prinz Heinrich Mütze*, which is basically a Greek fishing cap made of wool. In the south *Opas* might sport a Pinocchio-like *Alpenmütze* cap instead. Some *Omas* and *Opas* can be a bit crotchety since they lived through the Second World War, were POWs, and helped to rebuild their bombed-out country and all. So cut 'em some slack and give up your seat on the bus with a smile.

German grandmas and grandpas are totally cute.
***Omas und Opas** sind voll süß.*

CHAPTER 3

PARTY GERMAN
PARTY DEUTSCH

Despite their stereotype for being super punctual, hard-working clean-freaks, Germans love to party. The tips in this chapter will help you keep a cool head when getting your drink on, and distinguish between a *Vorglühen, Fest, Party, Feier,* and *Abtauparty*, even if you can't remember what happened when you were there.

▪▪▪▪▪It's party time!
Es wird gefeiert!

Like most people, when the average German leaves the office it's all play and no business, and they try to keep it that way. *Feierabend,* or "quitting time" in German, literally means "celebration evening," and it really is just that. When Germans get off work, the ties loosen, the formality disappears and the beer starts flowing. It's the perfect time for you to pick up on how your German friends and coworkers really talk and loosen up.

I wanna...
Ich will...

go downtown.
in die Stadt gehen.

go to the **club**.
*in die **Disko** gehen.*

get my groove on.
abhotten.

find a **hottie**.
*'ne geile **Schnitte** finden.*

meet up with friends.
ein paar Freunde treffen.

hook up with
a chick.
*ein Püppchen
abschleppen.*

hook up with
a dude.
***einen Kerl**
abschleppen.*

get some action.
was Action.

shag ass.
abhauen.

get home soon.
bald nach hause.

·····Whatta ya up to?
Was machste'?

No one, not even the serious and self-reliant Germans, really likes to party alone. So don't be shy about inviting your new German friends out. Next time you wanna scope out the action for the weekend, but don't know how to ask what your friends are up to, throw out a couple of these.

Whatta ya up to?
Was machste'?

> **Nuttin' much.**
> *Nüscht.* (used mostly in northern Germany)
>
> *Nischt.* (Sächsisch—from the east)
>
> *Nix.* (Bavarian, but works everywhere)
>
> **I'm bored out of my skull!**
> *Ich langweile mich zu Tode!*

Got any big plans for tonight?
*Haste' heute Abend **was Großartiges** vor?*

Whatta ya wanna do?
Was willste' denn machen?

> **Dunno, any suggestions?**
> *Weiß nicht, haste Vorschläge?*
>
> **Something cool.**
> *Was Cooles.*
>
> **Party hardy!**
> *Steil gehn!*

Are ya up for...
Haste' Bock auf...
Bock haben literally means "to have goat"

> **another beer?**
> *noch 'n Bierchen?*
>
> **somethin' to eat?**
> *was zu essen?*
>
> **barhopping?**
> *eine Kneipentour?*
>
> **smoking a fatty?**
> *dübeln?*

Bring it on!
Jetzt geht's los!

Hey, let's…
Hey, lass uns…

> **go out for a smoke.**
> *eine smöken gehen.*

> grab **the bong.**
> ***die Blubber** holen.*
> The name "*Blubber*" comes from the "blub blub" sound it
> makes when you smoke it.

> order **another round.**
> ***noch 'ne Runde** bestellen.*

> go to the **brothel!**
> *in den **Puff**!*

> **chill for a bit.**
> *mal chillen.*

> do some **crank calls.**
> ***Telefonterror** spielen.*

> **get nuts!**
> *auf die Katze treten!*
> Literally, "step on the cat"

·····Gettin' down!
Die Sau rauslassen!

Lass die Sau raus translates as "let the pig loose," and means
gettin' wild. But don't just scream it out like some drunken
fratboy letting everyone know that he's getting his drink on.
It's a German slang classic that is used loosely to describe the
mood for some seriously wild partying. Let your friends know
you're having a good time with some of these phrases.

> **Tonight…**
> *Heute abend…*

> > **we're gonna go wild.**
> > *lassen wir die Sau raus.*

> > I wanna party **like never before.**
> > *will ich feiern **wie noch nie zuvor**.*

I'm gonna get freaky on the dance floor!
worde ich auf der Tanzfläche richtig abspacken!
If used outside the context of dancing, it means to act like a dumb-ass, so watch out.

I'm ready for anything.
bin für jeden Scheiß bereit.

I'm gonna party all night!
werde ich durchfeiern!

I'm having a blast.
geht's mir glänzend.

I'm gonna raise the roof!
gebe ich richtig Gas!
Literally "step on the gas"

·····Chillin'
Chillen

Even hard-core partiers need a break every once in a while, and Germans are no different. Chillin' is so important to them that they even made up a new verb: *chillen*.

Tonight...
Heute Abend...

> **I just wanna hang out at home.**
> *will ich zuhause abhängen.*
>
> **I'm gonna chill on the couch.**
> *werde ich auf dem Sofa chillen.*
>
> **I'm gonna veg out.**
> *werde ich nur herumgammeln.*
> Literally, "to rot around"
>
> **I'm just gonna grab a pizza.**
> *hole mir 'ne Pizza.*
>
> **I feel like watching a video.**
> *will ich 'n Video gucken.*
>
> **I'm just gonna tug it and fall asleep.**
> *werde ich mir einen runterholen und einpennen.*

·····Party!
Es wird gefeiert!

Germans, like Eskimos and their infinite words for snow, seem to have a name for every type of party imaginable. Just slap "party" at the end of a noun or adjective and suddenly you have a whole new word to describe exactly how you're gonna get down. It's kinda like descriptions of porn: you've got scat porn, doggie porn, straight porn, gay porn, etc. Here are just a few examples of the types of parties you're likely to encounter.

Vorglühen

Vorglühen is literally what you do to a diesel motor to warm it up. So in slang it translates to pre-gaming or pre-funking—you know, the partying before the actual party. You usually start drinking at someone's house before a night out, or even on the way to the party. Drinking in public is allowed all over Germany, so buses, streetcars, trains, and corners are perfect spots for *vorglühen.*

Christian pre-gamed so hard that he didn't even make it to the party.
*Christian war schon beim **Vorglühen** total besoffen, dass er nicht zur Party gekommen ist.*

Semesteranfangsparty (f)

Students usually organize a "beginning-of-the-semester party," (or end-of-semester: *Semesterabschlußparty*) in one of the student housing complexes, which often come complete with a bar, dance floor, and enough outside space for a couple hundred of their fellow students to get hammered in. Different departments talk smack about how great their party will be. They're usually a bastion of drunken awesomeness, but if you choose the wrong one you'll get stuck with a bunch of awkward people standing around trying to sound smart.

Man, the business students throw the best end-of-semester parties!
Na, die BWL-er schmeißen wohl die besten ***Semesterabschlußpartys!***

Ballermann 6 party (f)

This is Germany's closest thing to spring break debauchery. Named after a popular beach bar on the Spanish island Mallorca, *Ballermann* parties can be small private parties or huge events in a club. Most attendees are there to relive their drunken nights at the actual *Ballermann* bar from a previous vacation. Just like in Mallorca, there's lots of cheesy pop music, beach attire, and sleazy guys looking to get into any girls' pants. Think of a Teutonic version of Cabo and you'll get the picture.

> **Thorsten got totally trashed at that Ballermann party and was ready to fuck anything that moved.**
> *Thorsten war auf der **Ballermannparty** vollblau und wollte egal was durchficken.*

Grillparty/Gartenparty (f)

Basically the German version of a backyard cookout. During bikini weather, anyone with a backyard *Garten* will invite friends over for a potluck-type bash with anything from *Sauerkraut* and *Schnitzel* to *Bratwürste* and beer.

> **Herms and Sabine are having a barbecue, but don't even think of bringing your crappy pasta salad.**
> *Freitag ist doch **Grillparty** bei Herms und Sabine, doch deinen eckligen Nudelsalat kannste vergessen.*

After-work-party (f)

This is basically happy hour. German clubs throw *After-work-partys* to attract young professionals between 6 and 10 p.m. Companies will even use them for "team-building," which is really just an excuse for a bunch of coworkers to get plastered together. But the Germans take this shit seriously. They have a phrase "*Dienst ist Dienst und Schnaps ist Schnaps,*" which means "duty is duty, and booze is booze." It's nice to see that they can keep their priorities straight.

> **At the after-work party I got completely hammered and made a pass at my boss.**
> *Auf der **After-work-party** war ich total besoffen und hab' den Chef angebaggert.*

Abtauparty (f)
This "thawing out party" isn't really a party at all, but the feeble attempt at recovering from your hangover with a little "hair of the dog that bit you."

> **Damn I feel like shit. I think need a little "hair of the dog."**
> *Mannomann ist mir schlecht. Ich brauch' 'ne **Abtauparty**.*

·····Where Germans hang out
Wo die Deutschen feiern

Kneipe (f)
Germany's answer to the pub; they're cozy and offer food and some entertainment in a laid-back, unpretentious environment. This is where most Germans go to have a beer, a bite to eat, and maybe listen to some live music and enjoy the atmosphere. It's the perfect place to end a hard day's work or begin a hard night's partying.

> **Wouldn't you rather just go to the pub instead of some shitty disco?**
> *Wolltest du nicht lieber in die **Kneipe** gehen, statt in die scheiß Disko?*

Disko (f)
These generic dance clubs can sometimes be cool, but are usually overrun by techno-loving teens and douchebags trying to bang Paris Hilton wannabes. Spend five minutes listening to shitty techno music in one of these places and you'll be ready to pour hot lead into your ears.

Man, these fucking discos drive me insane.
*Na also, diese Scheiß **Diskos** gehen mir echt auf den Sack.*

Club (m)

Less annoying than a *Disko* since this is where you'll see cool bands in a smaller setting. And getting to the bar is a whole lot less crowded, too.

The *Silke Arp Bricht* is coolest club in Hannover.
*Silke Arp Bricht ist der geilste **Club** in Hannover.*
(This club is one of the coolest I've been in. It's like an unpretentious indie arts collective with a bar. They've renovated the basement into a space for bands and dancing. The crowd is laid-back, the music is great, and the drinks are cheap. The founders describe it as a therapy center for hyperactive kids and it kinda is.)

Bar (f)

Plain old bars—which are strictly for booze and never offer food—are a bit of a rarity in Germany. Since Germans love to eat and dance when getting hammered, they usually only end up in one of these at the end of an evening out. More often than not it's a bar in a *Disko* or attached to a café. The Capri Bar in Bremen is a good one to check out if you get the chance—it's decked out like a cave inside.

Nah, the bar's boring. Let's go somewhere else instead.
*Nee, die **Bar** ist voll langweilig. Lass uns mal woanders hin.*

Lounge (f)

An ultra-trendy bar for people who'd rather get drunk sipping overpriced cocktails while sitting in expensive pieces of furniture than standing at a bar with a classic German beer.

Lounges are kinda faggy, but they're always swarming with hot chicks.
Also, die Bar ist doch etwas schwul, doch da gibt's immer heiße Mädels.

Gaststätte (e)/Gasthof (m)

There's no really good English translation for these, but they're closer to a restaurant than a pub, but with the laid-back atmosphere of a pub—kind of like an old school version of a gastropub. Though *Gaststätten* aren't particularly cool, go here when food is more important than booze and you don't want to lose your shirt on the bill.

> **The *Gaststätten* in this town are boring, but the food is really good.**
> *Die **Gaststätten** dieser Stadt sind voll langweilig, aber das Essen ist total lecker.*

Bahnhof (m)
There's something very liberating about getting sloshed in public with your friends while waiting for the last train home. Since you can drink in public, the train station is one of the best places for *Vorglühen* or even an *Abtauparty*.

> **Timm and I missed the last train, so we just got tanked at the train station and waited it out.**
> *Timm und ich haben den letzten Zug verpasst und kippten deshalb am **Bahnhof** ein paar Bierchen weg.*

Kiez (m)/Viertel (n)
The *Kiez* or *Viertel* is a general term for a cool district or neighborhood, like the French Quarter in New Orleans or the Village in New York, where there are tons of clubs, pubs, and restaurants. In Hamburg, the *Kiez* is St. Pauli, home to the infamous *Reeperbahn*, the red-light district known as The Sinful Mile, with its strip clubs, sex shops, and brothels.

> **Hey, wanna roll down to the Kiez and see what's going on?**
> *Wollen wir mal auf'n **Kiez** und die Lage abchecken?*

Rotlichtviertel (n)
Prostitution is alive and well in Germany. You'll find one of these red-light districts in pretty much any big city. In Hamburg it is a blocked off street in St. Pauli, conveniently next to a police station. In Düsseldorf, there's a building near the main train station or *Hauptbahnhof,* where the ladies of the evening sit in windows with their number on it, so you can pick one out before you even get off the train.

Who wants to head down to the brothel and get some?
*Wer will in den **Puff** und **bürsten**?*

Nutten gucken
Nutten gucken is a verb for groups of bored, drunk dudes who love to stop by the red-light district and check out the whores. It's like window-shopping for love, without catching an STD.

Dude, I'm fuckin' bored, let's go check out some sluts!
*Na Alda, mir ist strunzlangweilig, lass uns **Nutten gucken**!*

Go-Go Bar (f)
This isn't a nudie bar, just a bunch of scantily clad chicks dancing and serving really expensive drinks. The beer might cost you twenty dollars but the blue balls are free.

I'm sick of all those cockteases at the go-go bar.
*Von den Flittchen in der **Go-Go Bar** habe ich's echt satt.*

Stripclub (m)/Striplokal (n)
A straight up titty bar. These can usually be found near a *Bahnhof* or in the *Rotlichtviertel.* You'd think that legal brothels would make these kind of obsolete, but businessmen and bachelor parties can't seem to get enough of 'em.

I blew my whole paycheck at the titty bar. My wife's gonna kill me!
*Das ganze Geld habe ich im **Stripclub** weggeschmissen. Meine Alte bringt mich um!*

Stadtfest/Schützenfest/Fest (n) or Kirmes (f)
Kinda like a county fair, but with better food, fewer ex-con carny folk, and more drunks. Each year, every city will have at least one of these things, usually around a holiday. They're like mini Oktoberfests with all of the beer but none of the lame-ass tourists. If you get a chance, check out a *Schützenfest*. It's fuckin' nuts! It's a huge party held after a massive shooting

competition…that's right: drunk Germans with big-ass guns.

> **Let's go to the fair. I wanna get sloshed and ride the roller coaster.**
> *Lass uns mal zum **Stadtfest**. Ich will **saufen** und Achterbahn fahren.*

·····Booze
Alkohol

At first glance, Germans might seem like a bunch of drunks, because booze is everywhere: bars, restaurants, corner shops, train stations, food kiosks. Even the golden arches sells beer. Beer is definitely the Fatherland's most popular social lubricant, but Germans also drink a shitload of wine and, of course, *Schnaps*. But whatever you're drinking, there are a few phrases you'll need to know to help ease you into inebriation.

Wanna drink?
Willste was trinken?

Whatta ya got to drink?
*Was gibt's zu **trinken**?*

To toast
anstossen (look everyone in the eye when toasting, otherwise you'll be cursed with bad sex)

> **Should we make a toast?**
> *Sollten wir nicht **anstoßen**?*

Cheers!
Prost!

Less talkin', more drinkin'!
Nicht lang schnacken, Kopp im Nacken!
In Northern Germany, literally, "cut the chatter, tip your head into your neck."

Here's to...
Auf...

> **getting plastered!**
> *breit werden!*

> **all my old girlfriends (boyfriends)! May they burn in Hell!**
> *meine Ex-freundinnen (Ex-freunde)! Mögen sie in der Hölle schmoren!*

> **unemployment!**
> *die Arbeitslosigkeit!*

> **alcohol poisoning!**
> *Alkoholvergiftung!*

To your health!
Zum Wohl! (normally used just with wine or *Schnaps*)

Down the hatch!
Prösterchen!

·····Beer
Bier

Beer is to Germans what wine is to the Italians, cheese is to the French and child abuse is to the Belgians. If you don't like beer, you'll be kind of an outcast in Germany.

> **What's on tap?**
> *Was gibt's vom Fass?*

> **Do you only have beer in bottles?**
> *Habt ihr nur Flaschenbier?*
> Most *Kneipen*, *Bars* and *Gaststätten* have regional beers and maybe a larger national one on tap, while clubs usually stick to bottles.

> **Hey guys, what's the local beer?**
> *Hey Jungs, was ist denn das Regionalbier?*

Hey, how's about we go out tonight and crack a few cold ones.
*Mensch, lass uns heute Abend **ein kühles Blondes zischen** gehen.*

So, what's the deal with this beer purity law?
*Also, was ist mit dem **Reinheitsgebot**?*
A nineteenth-century national law limited beer's ingredients to water, barley, and hops to ensure purity. You'll still see "brewed according to the national purity law" on plenty of beers today.

Hey, wanna bust out the beer-bong?
*Na, wollen wir **trichtern**?*
Literally to "do the funnel"

What the fuck, you've only got shit-beer?
*Was soll das denn, nur **Aldi-beer**?*
Aldi is a cheap grocery store with crappy beer.

Hey, I'm goin' to grab some brews, ya want one?
*Na, ich geh mal **Bierchen** holen, soll ich dir was mitbringen?*

Drink! Drink! Drink!
Heu! Heu! Heu!
Someone yells "*Zicke Zicke Zicke Zacke!*" [don't ask why] then everyone shouts back "*Heu! Heu! Heu!*", and then everyone drinks! drinks! drinks!

GERMAN BEERS)))

MÄRZEN-OKTOBERFESTBIER (n)

This deep amber lager is the official beer of Oktoberfest and is brewed only by breweries within Munich's city limits in the springtime (*März* means "March"). By the time these beers make it to the Oktoberfest, they've been aged in caves and have an alcohol content of like six percent. *Prost!*

HEFEWEIZEN (m)

Unfiltered wheat beer which is hugely popular in the south. If you're getting trashed in a *Biergarten* in Bavaria, it's probably on this.

KRISTALLWEIZEN (m)

The filtered version of a Hefeweizen and generally popular with girls and effeminate men.

KÖLSCH (n)

A pale, light-bodied, but high in alcohol beer which can only legally be brewed in and around Köln (Cologne). It will kick your ass.

SCHWARZBIER (n)

Similar to a *Rauchbier*, or smoked beer, it's a really dark lager beer with a full, smoky, almost chocolatey flavor. Similar to Guinness or any other stout, but since it isn't a stout, it's less heavy. Köstritzer is the best.

BOCKBIER (n)

It's an amber, heavy-bodied, bittersweet lager named after a male goat. Drink enough and it feels like one rammed you in the head.

PILSNER (ALSO PILS) (m)

Really the most popular beer. It's a light-bodied, hoppy beer (the bitterness depends on the brewery) which everyone drinks year round. Since it's available throughout the country all the time, try out some different regional versions for a real beer tour of Germany. Jever from the north is really hoppy and bitter. Radeberger and Wernesgrüner are from the old East Germany; both are now widely available and amazing.

BERLINER WEISSE (MIT SCHUSS)

This pale, very sour, wheat beer is brewed in Berlin. It's so sour you'll usually drink it mixed with a shot (*Schuss*) of either Raspberry (red) or Waldmeister (green) syrup. Waldmeister tastes like liquid cotton candy, so take the appropriate precautions.

·····Hard alcohol
Schnaps (m)

In just about any German *Kneipe* you'll see a couple of *Underberg Belts* hanging from behind the bar. These things look like Pancho Villa's bullet belt, but instead of holding bullets, they hold twenty little bottles of Underberg, an herb-based aperitif. The belts are mostly just for decoration, but when you get two dumb-asses drunk enough to challenge each other to *Wettsaufen* (competition drinking), the belts come down and the first person to get alcohol poisoning wins.

You wanna have a go at the Underberg Belts?
*Sollten wir mal **den Gürtel** holen?*

A shot
Schuss (m)

A double
Doppel
Combine it with your favorite booze: *Doppelvodka*, *Doppelwhisky*, etc.

On the rocks
auf Eis
Even just "on the rocks" in a really cool German accent will work.

Straight up
Pur

The well brand
Hausmarke (f)/des Hauses
Always used in conjunction with your alcohol of choice: *Whisky des Hauses*, *Vodka des Hauses*, etc.

Schnaps is just a generic term for hard alcohol, but here are some classic fuck-you-up favorites:

Obstbrand (m): *Schnaps* made from fruit wine, but not just for chicks.

Korn (m): 60-proof grain alcohol that tastes like paint thinner unless mixed with something else.

Doppelkorn (m): 80-proof *Korn* and even worse tasting.

Magenbitter (m): "Stomach bitters" is an aperitif, but most people knock it back in shots. Jägermeister and Underberg are the most well-known brands. Too many of these and you're on your way to a coma.

Bommerlunder (m): A German "Aquavit" type of licorice-flavored booze that's usually served in chilled shots and has even inspired a drinking song from German punk band *Die Toten Hosen*. Be sure to sing both of these verses at increasing speed until you can't sing any faster or you puke your drunk-ass guts out, whichever comes first.

Eisgekühlter Bommerlunder -
Bommerlunder eisgekühlt.
Eisgekühlter Bommerlunder -
Bommerlunder eisgekühlt.

Und dazu:
Ein belegtes Brot mit Schinken - Schinken!
Ein belegtes Brot mit Ei - Ei!
Das sind zwei belegte Brote,
eins mit Schinken uns eins mit Ei.

Ice cold Bommerlunder-
Bommerlunder, ice cold.
Ice cold Bommerlunder-
Bommerlunder, ice cold.

and then:
A little sandwich with ham – Ham!
A little sandwich with eggs – Eggs!
You've a couple of little sandwiches,
one with ham and one with eggs.

DRINKING SONGS)))
SAUFLIEDER

Germans love to sing drinking songs when they're getting hammered in beer tents and at fairs. There are lots of traditional classics, but they'll usually latch onto whatever shitty pop song fits with getting shitfaced. Sometimes the song is actually good and becomes a classic in its own right, like this song *Sauflied* by the German punk band *Die Ärzte*.

> *Ich und meine Kumpels, wir sind ein duftes Team*
> *Wir sind regelrechte Alkoholvernichtungsmaschin'*
> *Wir saufen bis zum Umfall'n, alle machen mit*
> *Und wenn wir dann besoffen sind, dann sing' wir unser Lied*
>
> *Komm, wir grölen noch ein bißchen, denn ich bin schon wieder voll*
> *Komm, wir singen übers Saufen, über Bier und Alkohol.*

Me and all of my buddies, we're a bad-ass horde
We're a bunch of alcohol burning machines
We drink until we fall down and everyone's on board
and whenever we get fucked up, this is what we sing

Come on let's get loud in here, cuz my belly's getting full
Come and sing about drinkin', 'bout beer and alcohol.

•••••Gettin' blitzed
breit werden

Wanna toss back a couple cold ones?
Wollen wir ein paar Bierchen wegkippen?

I'm...
Ich...

> **buzzed.**
> *bin gut drauf.*
>
> **gettin' tipsy.**
> *werde etwas beschwipst.*
>
> **drunk.**
> *bin ganz schön betrunken.*

wasted.
besoffen.

smashed.
bin total angeschickert.

getting really fucking hammered.
werde vollbreit.
Literally, "getting wide"

drunk off my ass.
bin total lattenstramm.
Literally, "laid out like planks of wood"

I'm **drunk as a skunk.**
*Ich bin so **breit wie ein Biberschwanz**.*
Literally, "as wide as a beaver's tail"

I'm kinda **dizzy.**
*Mir wird's **schwindelig**.*

I'm gonna be sick.
Mir wird's schlecht.

I'm think I'm gonna **ralph.**
*Ich muss mit **Jörg telefonieren**.*
Literally, "to call Jörg." Like Ralph, Jörg is a name that sounds like puking.

VOMITOLOGY)))
KOTZOLOGIE

I GOTTA...	ICH MUSS...
vomit	*mich erbrechen*
puke	*kotzen*
throw up	*mich übergeben*
barf	*göbeln*
blow chunks	*den Döner abwürfeln*
hurl	*kübeln*
spew	*reihern*
yak	*abbröckeln*

Dude, tell me how I ended up in bed with your mom, I totally blacked out.
*Mensch ich **habe voll den Filmriss**, wie bin ich mit deiner Mutter im Bett gelandet.*
Like when the film is missing a scene

I've got the worst hangover.
*Ich habe voll den **Affen**.*
Literally, "to have an ape"

He's a total drinking machine.
*Er ist ein echter **Kampftrinker**.*

He can barely stand up!
*Der Typ da **nimmt schon Bodenprobe**!*
Literally, "taking samples of the floor"

Man, you can barely walk straight.
*Alter, du bist ja voll **kursiv unterwegs**.*
Literally, "walking cursively"

She's so drunk, she's just muttering bullshit to strangers.
*Die ist so dicht, dass sie die **Muttersprache verloren hat**.*
Literally, "losing your mother tongue"

You're a total alcoholic.
*Du bist voll **der Alkomat**.*

Germans are the coolest drunks.
*Die Deutschen sind die coolsten **Säufer**.*

·····Weed
Gras

German law regarding weed is weird. It's sorta decriminalized, meaning they won't pop you just for being high. But you can't buy, sell, grow, hold or distribute weed, though seeds are

OK. Even little cities have head/grow shops (*Headshops/ Growshops*). They sell everything from papers (*Blättchen*) to bongs (*Bongs*) to pipes (*Pfeifen*) and hookahs (*Wasserpfeifen*). And just like when you're looking to score in the States, you only want to talk about it with those who smoke. Don't just walk into a shop and ask 'em where you can get the stickiest of the icky. But, if you play it cool, you'll find plenty of friends who are holdin'.

Germany borders Holland, so there's a steady supply of high-quality shit right next door, which by default spills over the border. Most cops in big cities overlook pot and focus on hard drugs. But Bavarian cops can be hard-asses about it. They often target backpackers who wanna hit the bong before hitting the Oktoberfest. German stoner-speak uses tons of English terms, but your buds (pun intended) will definitely have their own code words for all things cheeba.

Dude, I need to get baked.
*Hay, ich will nach **Maryland fahren**.*
Literally, "drive to Mary (Jane) land"

Hey, wanna smoke some hash?
*Na, wollen wir **einen harzen**?*
Harzen means "to exude resin"

I ain't gotta piece.
*Kein **Fuckel**.*

It's time to roll that shit!
*Na los, **aufwickeln**!*

Sorry bra, I barely got enough for a pinner.
*Sorry Alter, das hier reicht nicht mal für **einen Sticky**.*

Roller's rights!
Wer baut, der haut!

Can you really get some kind Amsterdam bud?
*Kannste' wirklich was **Dutch** besorgen?*

Holy shit man, you never hit the gravity bong before? It's the bomb!
*Bhoa Digga, niemals **Eimer geraucht**? Ist doch voll geil!*
Literally, "smoke the bucket"

I've never seen a spliff that big before, it's like a baby arm!
*So 'ne **Tüte** habe ich noch nie gesehen, die ist doch riesig!*
Tüte is short for the giant cone-shaped Schultüte filled with candy and presents German kids get on their first day of school.

I'm jones-ing for a joint right now.
Ich hab' voll Bock auf 'ne Sportzigarette.

Will you show me how to roll a blunt?
*Zeigst du mir wie man **eine** rollt?*

Let's hotbox the bathroom.
*Lass uns auf dem Klo **hotboxen**.*

I'm so high right now.
*Ich bin total **bekifft**.*

FIELDS OF GREEN)))
BLÜHENDE LANDSCHAFTEN

Weed	Weed
Hash	Haschisch
Bud	Pott
Chronic	Chronic
Reefer	Shit
Mary Jane	Maryland
Green	was Grünes (literally, "some green")
Ganja	Ganja
Grass	Gras

Check him out, man, he's totally faded.
*Hey guck mal, der ist voll **benebelt**.*
Literally, "fogged up"

Wanna get somethin' to eat? I totally got the munchies.
*Willste was essen? Ich hab' voll **den Fresskick**.*

Bro, you're such a pothead.
*Na Alda, du bist ja voll der **Kiffer**.*

·····Hard drugs
Harte Drogen

I don't need to say that cocaine is a helluva drug; just ask Rick James. Oh wait. You can't. That shit killed him. German cops take hard drugs pretty seriously and will throw your ass in prison for a long haul if they catch you with any. But you'll still see plenty of junkies and crackheads at the train and subway stations in Frankfurt.

Know where I can score some...
Wo kriege ich was...

No thanks...ain't my thing.
Nee...ist nichts für mich.

> **Coke**
> *Koks (m)*
>
> **Crack**
> *Crack (m)*
>
> **Heroin**
> *Heroin (n)*
>
> **Shrooms**
> *Fliegepilze (pl)*
> Literally, "flying mushrooms"
>
> **Ecstasy**
> *Extasy (n)*

Pills
Pillen (pl)

Meth
Meth

Acid
LSD

Get away from me, you **junky**.
*Hey du **Junky**, hau ab.*

That guy ain't nothing but a **cokehead**.
*Der Typ da ist voll der **Koksnase**.*

Whoa, that dude's **covered in track marks**!
*Bhoa, der da ist **voll der Kanülen-Pete**!*

BODY GERMAN
KÖRPER DEUTSCH

•••••Sexy Germans
Sexy Deutsche

Let's face it, the last time Germans thought too much about the ideal German, they got themselves and the rest of the world into a shitload of trouble. Nowadays sexiness is pretty much universal, and the average German's take on hotness is no different than the average American's. Most people on both sides of the pond think Heidi Klum, Halle Berry, and Brad Pitt are hot, but wouldn't fuck Rosanne Barr with a stolen dick.

She's/He's...
Sie/Er ist...

> **kinda tall.**
> *etwas größer.*

> **charming.**
> *charmant.*

> **cute.**
> *hübsch.* (mostly for girls and kinda gay for guys)

> **pretty.**
> *schön.* (for girls)

handsome.
herrlich. (for guys)

gorgeous.
hinreißend.

hot.
scharf.

ripped.
muskelbepackt.

tan.
gebräunt.

cool.
cool.

stylish.
modisch.

sporty.
sportlich.

slim.
schlank.

well-groomed/put together.
gepflegt.

popular with the guys/girls.
beliebt bei den Jungs/Mädchen.

She's/He's got…
Sie/Er hat…

a cute smile.
ein schönes Lächeln.

beautiful eyes.
wunderschöne Augen.

a great face.
ein tolles Gesicht.

a toned figure.
eine sportliche Figur.

a great attitude/aura.
eine nette Ausstrahlung.

a firm ass.
'nen knackigon Arsch

I'm lookin' for a girl who got some junk in da trunk.
Ich brauch' 'n Mädel mit 'ner Ködelkiste.

I guess you can't really get a six-pack just by drinking 'em, can you?
Mann kriegt warscheinlich kein Waschbrett vom Saufen, oder?

Dude, you're built like Arnold!
Mensch, du bist echt der Arnie!

•••••Ugly Germans
Hässliche Deutsche

Spend enough time in Germany and you'll quickly see that not everyone looks like a Nordic god. Unfortunately, the land that blessed the world with Heidi Klum and Claudia Schiffer also kicked us in the sack with Siegfried and Roy. In Germany, it's not polite to stare and make jokes about the hideously ugly, so wait until Frankenstein's monster has left before you ridicule him or her to your friends.

She's/He's...
Sie/Er ist...

> **kinda short.**
> *etwas kleiner.*
>
> **awkward.**
> *ungeschickt.*
>
> **boring.**
> *langweilig.*

unattractive.
reizlos.

ugly.
hässlich.

nasty.
grässlich.

not too stylish.
unmodisch.

not very sporty.
unsportlich.

chubby.
pummelig.

husky.
kräftig.

fat.
fett.

sloppy/disheveled.
ungepflegt.

not too popular with the guys/girls.
unbeliebt bei Jungs/Mädchen.

cross-eyed.
shielt.

fugly.
ein echtes Gesichtsdresden.
Dresden was bombed flat in the Second World War, so this is pretty fuckin' ugly.

butt-white.
voll das Kellerkind.
Literally, "cellar-kid," like a video game junky

a tub o' lard.
ein Fettbatzen.

a bean pole.
ein langer Lulatsch.
Refers to the radio tower in Berlin

an Amazon/a giant chick.
eine Amazone.

tiny.
Zwerg-mäßig.
Literally, "gnomish"

kinda wimpy.
ein Sitzpinkler.
One who pisses sitting down; an insult just for dudes

sort of a hunchback.
etwas buckelig.

She's/He's got…
Sie/Er hat…

a crooked smile.
ein kaputtes Lächeln.

dumbo ears.
Segelohren. (ears like sails)

bug-eyes.
Glubschaugen.

love-handles.
Griffe am Arsch.
Literally, "ass-handles" here

some serious plumber's crack.
echt das Bauarbeiter-Dekolleté.
Literally, "construction worker cleavage"

stinky feet.
Käsemauken. (like a stinky cheese)

Should I get lipo?
*Sollte ich mir mal etwas **Fett absaugen lassen**?*

Whoa baby, you got some hairy pits, shave that shit!
*Bhoa, das ist voll der **Achselfasching**, rasier dich mal!*

I'm starting to get a beer belly.
*Ich kriege langsam 'nen **Waschtrommelbauch**.*
Like a washtub

·····Farting
Furzen

Most normal Germans will be discreet and excuse themselves to go drop an air biscuit. Your friends, however, are not normal people and will bust ass right in front of you…and then catch it and buttercup your unsuspecting face with it. When you take into account that the stereotypical German diet consists of beer, cheese, and sausage, you'll be amazed that the whole country doesn't go up in flames every time someone lights a cigarette. So thank God the Germans are slowly banning smoking in enclosed public spaces.

A fart
Furz (m)

To fart
furzen

To pass gas
blähen

To toot
pupsen

I just…
Ich habe gerade…

> **floated an air biscuit.**
> *einen **Luftkeks** gebacken.*
> Literally, "baked an air cookie" reserved for fluffy airy ones

> **dropped a bomb.**
> *habe den Koffer stehen lassen.*
> Literally, "left the suitcase"

> **whistled out my ass.**
> *auf die Darmflöte gespielt.*
> Often a high-pitched squeaker, like playing the intestinal flute

Hey, hold your breath, I'm gonna **crack one off.**
*Eh, Luft anhalten, ich muss **einen abdrücken.***

You just **bust ass?**
*Haste' **gefurzt?***

Hey man it wasn't me, must have been a **barking spider.**
*Hey ich war's nicht, wir haben **Brüllmücken** im Haus.*
Literally, "roaring mosquitos"

Dude, why you always **lettin' 'em rip?**
*Eh, warum musst du ständig **einen ziehen lassen?***

Hey **butt-trumpet,** quit farting!
*Hey du **Arschpfeife,** hör auf zu pupsen!*

Franz loves to smell his own farts. He's the king of the **Dutch oven.**
*Franz liebt den Geruch seiner eigenen Furzen. Er ist voll der **Gaskragen** freak.*
Literally, "a fart-collar"

I hear you can singe your ass hair off by **lighting your farts.**
*Hab' mal gehört, dass man bei einem **Afterburner** die Arschhaare absengt.*

I think that one's gonna leave some **skidmarks.**
*Die Nummer wird aber **Bremsstreifen** hinterlassen.*

Your girlfriend ever busted a **queef** on you?
*Hat deine freundin schon 'ne richtige **Muschifurz** auf dich los gelassen?*

FOREIGNER'S FIELD GUIDE TO FARTING)))

SCHURZ (m)

A cross between *Scheiße* and *Furz*, but specifically describes a really wet fart. It rhymes with the "squirts" so it shouldn't be too hard to remember.

PUPS MIT PELLE (m)

The "solid" cousin of the aforementioned *Schurz*, this is literally a "fart with a skin." Think of it as coughing a hairball out of your ass. The emphasis here is on the fact that the shit coming out was accidental.

L.A.T. (LEISE ABER TÖDLICH) (m)

A straight up "silent but deadly." The SBD is kinda like the land mine of farts ... you don't see it coming until you've walked right into it.

AFTERHUSTEN

Attacks of "ass sneezing" can be of various lengths, loudness, and intensity ... just like regular sneezing, only you don't wanna be around to say *Gesundheit*!

UFO (UNBESTIMMBARES FURZENDES OBJEKT) (n)

An "unidentified farting object." For those ghost farts when no one knows who dealt it, but everyone can smell it. Most Germans won't admit to blowing ass, so you'll probably have plenty of these close encounters of the farting kind.

GRANATENWURF (m)

The German "grenade toss" is equivalent to the "cup and throw" or "buttercup" techniques practiced in locker rooms across the U.S. Basically, you fart into your cupped hand and strategically throw the result into the face of your victim. The key to the *Granatenwurf* is all in the throw: too slow and your "grenade" loses its power, too fast and it could slip through your fingers. Performed properly, your fart will be sure to linger in your buddy's goatee for a while.

·····Shitting
scheißen

I don't know about you, but for me, takin' a dump in a public restroom can be pretty traumatic. In Germany, though, public shitting is a thing of beauty. Most public restrooms have attendants who keep things squeaky clean, unlike those diarrhea-blasted holes they call toilets in Spain. Going even further, a select handful of German train stations are home to the McClean, the *Neuschwannstein* of German shithouses. These graffiti-free, designer poop palaces have automatically opening frosted-glass entrances, no-touch flushes and faucets, air fresheners, classical music, and are always as clean and sparkly as that chick's teeth in those Orbit gum ads. They're so inviting that never again will you be afraid to drop a deuce in public.

I gotta...
Ich muss mal...

> **poop.**
> *kacken.*

> **shit.**
> *scheißen.*

> **take a dump.**
> *einen abseilen.*
> Literally, "to lower one down on a rope"

> **take a crap.**
> *böllern.*

A turd
Kacke (f)

A pile of shit
Scheißhaufen (m)

Diarrhea
Flitzekacke (f)

I need to go poo-poo.
Ich muss A-A machen. (kinda cutesy)

I gotta go pinch a loaf.
Ich muss ja einen abkneifen.

It's time to drop the kids off at the pool.
Ich muss Bob in die Bahn werfen.
Literally, to throw "Bob" onto the train

Hang on a sec, I just gotta pound one out.
Moment mal, muss nur noch 'ne Stange Lehm aus'm Kreuz leiern.
Literally, "to churn a stick of mud out of your spine"

Yesterday it was like I was peeing outta my butt!
Gestern musste ich schon wieder arschpissen!

This morning I had a major hangover and some serious beer shits too!
Heute morgen war ich voll verkatert und hatte auch Gumobischi dazu!

Drunk Germans love nothing more than inventing new words by stringing together a bunch of other words and then abbreviating them. *Gumobischi* is one such abbreviation, short for *Guten Morgen Bierschiss*—the "good morning beer shit" you experience when mud starts raining out of your butt the morning after a night of heavy drinking.

That was a real ring stinger!
Das war voll der Rosettenbrand!

I'm pretty backed up.
Ich bin ja voll verstopft.

Aaaaaah! That felt like I was shitting boulders.
Mann Mann Mann! Das war voll der Brikettschiss.

**Ulrich shaves his ass, otherwise he gets dingle
berries.**
*Der Ulrich rasiert sich den After, sonst kreigt er
Klabusterbeeren.*

That's way too much fuckin' information.
*Echt **zu viele fucking Infos**.*

Hey, where're the shit tickets?
*Wo steckt denn die **Böllerpappe**?*

Holy fuck, did someone die in here?
*Scheiße eh, **liegt hier 'n toter Esel inner Ecke**, oder
was?*

No bathroom stall would be complete without some shit-
themed wisdom. Here are a couple of gems I've actually seen
scrawled in German shithouses:

> *Gut gefurzt ist halb geschissen!*
> A good fart is like half a dump!

> *Wem die Scheiße bis zum Hals steht, sollte den Kopf
> nicht hängen lassen.*
> When you're up to your neck in shit, make sure to keep
> your chin up.

·····Pissing
Pissen

Lots of German urinals have a little fly painted on the inside
of the bowl for guys to use as a target. It's close enough
to the drain and set at just the right angle so if you hit the
fly you don't get any dreaded backsplash. It's kinda hard to
concentrate when you're completely blotto, but it still helps
prevent you from pissing on your Adidas. How's that for
German engineering?

Pee
Pipi (n)

Piss
Pisse (f)

Urine
Urin (m)

I gots to go.
Ich muss mal.

I gotta pee again already.
*Ich muss schon **wieder Pipi machen**.*

I'm gonna go take a leak.
*Ich geh' mal **austreten**.*
Literally, "to step out of formation"

That dude just whizzed in the pool!
*Der Typ hat eben gerade ins Becken **gepinkelt**!*

Uh-oh, terror alert level has been raised to yellow!
*Oh-oh, **Alarmstufe Gelb**!*

Do you get the piss shivers too?
***Zitterst** du auch beim **Pullern**?*

How are you supposed to take a leak when you wake up with a major piss-boner?
*Wie kannste schiffen wenn du mit 'ner **ChroMoPiLa** aufwachst?*
ChroMoPiLa is short for *Chronische Morgenpisslatte*. The need to piss is what distinguishes this from the regular "morning wood" or *AlMoPraLa*—All morgentliche Prachtlatte.

I think I'm gonna take a piss here in the bushes.
*Ich geh' mal hinter'm Gebusche **schiffen**.*

Hey, how about pissing for distance?
*Na, wie wär's mit **Wettpissen**?*

Do German chicks always go **pee in groups** like American girls?
*Sind alle deutsche Mädchen **Rudelpisser**, wie die amerikanischen Mädels?*

•••••Assorted bodily fluids and oddities
Körperflüssigkeiten und Anderes

Popel (m) or "booger" is an extremely useful word. It's used as a compound noun for eye-boogers and earwax as well as its own verb. Germans are totally cool with picking their nose (or almost any other orifice) in public so don't be surprised if mid-conversation someone starts pickin' some nose gold, rolls it up, and drops it on the floor without even pausing to say excuse me. Here are a few phrases to express your disgust with your friends' filthy behavior.

Dude, quit **picking your nose**!
*Mensch, hör auf zu **popeln**!*

Go ahead and **wipe that on your shirt**.
*Na los denn, einfach **auf dein Hemd aufstreichen**.*

Check out that kid, he's totally **nose drilling**.
*Schau mal, der Typ **bohrt voll in die Nase**.*

Hey, is your **nose gold** salty, too?
*Schmeckt auch dein **Nasengold** salzig?*

Wipe up your **snot**!
*Wisch dir den **Schnotten** ab!*

You got a Kleenex?
Haste mal 'n Tempos?
Tempos is the major German brand of tissue.

I caught him eating his boogers.
Den habe ich beim Popelfressen erwischt.

Fuck, man, my nose ring is all infected and oozing puss.
Scheiße ähh, mein Nasenring ist voll infiziert und vereitert.

Can you pop this zit for me?
Kannst du mir mal diesen Pickel platzen?

I get insane nosebleeds when I'm drunk.
Ich kriege voll die Nasenblutung, wenn ich besoffen bin.

Why do you always smell your earwax?
Wiseo musst du denn deinen Ohrenpopel riechen?

I slept so long my eyelids got glued shut with eye-boogers.
Ich hab so lange geschlafen, dass meine Augenlider mit Augenpopel zugeklebt waren.

I've never seen dick cheese before.
Nillenkäse habe ich noch nie live gesehen.

I've got this nasty whitehead on my butt cheek.
Ich habe voll den Packel auf meiner Arschbacke.

He was a total pizza face in high school.
In der Schule, war er voll die Gesichtspizza.

She didn't tell me that she was on the rag.
Sie hat mir nicht gesagt, dass sie ihre Tage hatte.

⁘General sickness
Übelkeit

Germans love to talk about how sick they are, and will go see a doctor at the slightest sign of a cold. Maybe it's cuz they're a bunch of whiny hypochondriacs, or maybe it's because their healthcare system kicks the American healthcare system in the taco. Anyway, I slammed my thumb in a car door and got patched up for like five bucks, so I'm not complaining.

I'm feeling kinda yucky.
*Mir ist **schlecht**.*

Man, you're lookin' pretty shitty.
*Mensch, du **siehst aber scheiße aus**.*

I'm not doin' so hot today.
*Heute **geht's mir nicht so gut**.*

You're looking a little pale.
*Du siehst aber **blass** aus.*

I just puked my guts out.
*Ich **ließ mir das Essen durch den Schädel gehen**.*
Literally, "to let your food out through your skull"

I've got leprosy and my nipples are falling off.
*Ich habe **Lepra** und mir fallen die Brustwarzen ab.*

Call an ambulance damn it!
*Ruf doch den **Krankenwagen**!*
A German ambulance is literally "the sick wagon"

I need some drugs!
*Ich brauche **Drogen**!*

I'm stayin' home from work today. **I got a cold.**
*Ich geh heute nicht zur Arbeit. **Ich hab'***
Schnodderseuche.

I've got…
Ich habe…

> **a headache.**
> *Gehirnmauke. (pl)*
> Literally, "a withering, aging brain"

> **a stomachache.**
> *Magenschmerzen. (pl)*

> **the flu.**
> *'ne Grippe. (f)*

> **crabs.**
> *Sackratten. (pl)*

> **herpes.**
> *Herpes. (m)*

> **a serious hangover.**
> *Schädelfrass. (m)* (like moths eating away at your skull)

> **a case of the clap.**
> *voll die Rüsselseuche.* (really the sniffles, but here it's
> running outta your cock)

> **a visit from Aunt Flo.** (i.e., a heavy-flow day)
> *Besuch von Tante Ruth.*
> In Germany, it's your Aunt Ruth who comes a callin' once a
> month, not your Aunt Flo.

·····Hair
Haar

OK, I know what you're thinking…German women don't
shave. But the days of the hairy-legged *Fräulein* are long
gone, and it's really only stinky hippies and other nasty chicks
you wouldn't wanna see naked anyway who are still goin'
Sasquatch. Nowadays, there's nothing a German woman
wouldn't shave. But a lot of Krauts do still have some weird-

ass body hair and some hilarious ways to describe it. Here are a few to look out for.

Achseldackel (m)
Extremely hairy armpits.
Literally, "an armpit Dachshund"

Alfstrumpfhose (f)
Remember that awesomely shitty TV show *ALF*? He was a hairy little alien that for some reason the Germans were, and still are, crazy about. So if your legs are insanely hairy, you've got "Alf socks."

O-li-ba (m)
Short for *Ober-Lippen-Bart* or "upper lip beard." Moustaches suck, so make fun of dudes who have 'em, especially hipsters who think mustaches are funny and ironic (hint: they're not; they're just ugly).

Vo-ku-hi-la (m)
Means short in the front (**vo**rne **ku**rz), long in the back (**hi**nten **la**ng). You may call it a mullet, hair cape, or Kentucky waterfall, and think it looks like hillbilly shit, but certain Germans love this style. Extremely popular among *Prolls* and *Rockers* (see Chapter Two "Friendly German").

Geburtsrahmen (m)
Literally, a "birth frame." Ever notice how a full beard resembles the "beard" babies get when coming out of their mama?

Gesichtsfotze (f)
If you think about it, "face-pussy" is a pretty perfect description of a goatee.

Bauklammer (m)
A moustache that looks like the giant construction staple for which it's named. Think of a "BGM" or Hulk Hogan's walrus 'stache.

Silberrücken (m)
This description of insane back hair is taken from "Silverback" gorillas…the name says it all.

Brustpullover (m)
Think of a sweater made out of chest hair.

HORNY GERMAN
GEILES DEUTSCH

•••••Fucking
Ficken

Germans are known throughout the world as über-geeks because of their fascination with order and accuracy. Geeky order-freaks they may be, but Germans *still* love to fuck. That doesn't mean that their slang for fucking isn't subject to order and accuracy, however. For instance, some Germans will actually describe sex as "sticking your pissing utensils together." Now that's German precision, baby!

Are you as horny as I am?
Bist du so geil wie ich?

I'm totally hot for you, let's...
Ich bin super heiß auf dich, wollen wir mal...

Let's go to my place and...
Lass uns zu mir gehen und...

Do you wanna talk all night or...?
Willst du mich volllabern, oder...?

> **hump**
> *poppen* (silly)
>
> **fuck**
> *ficken*
>
> **fuck like bunnies**
> *wie Kanninchen rammeln*
>
> **do it**
> *es tun*
>
> **have a quickie**
> *einen Quickie haben*
>
> **hit it/bone**
> *bocken/hämmern/nageln*
>
> **lay some pipe**
> *das Rohr verlegen*
>
> **screw**
> *vögeln*
>
> **bump uglies**
> *das Pissgeschirr zusammen stecken*
> Literally, "to stick our pissing utensils together"

Wanna have sex on the rag?
Willst du ins rote Meer stechen?

You can fuck me in the ass!
Mir kannst du die Muffe vergolden!

·····Genitalia, etc.
Schämikalien

Goethe is known as Germany's greatest poet and philosopher, but he was also an anatomist. He discovered the intermaxillary bone, which in German historical importance ranks just behind the invention of the printing press, the Protestant reformation, and the mass production of Oktoberfest mugs.

What does Goethe's "bone" mean to you? Well, it links your investigation of human anatomy to a great philosopher and makes you seem like less of a perv for wanting to say "Lick my *Knackmumu*."

Lick my…!
Leck mein- (-e, -en)…!

Stroke my…!
Streichel mein- (-e, -en)…!

Suck my…!
Saug/Lutsch mein- (-e, -en)…!

Slap my…!
Schlag mein- (-e, -en)…!

I love…(your)
Ich liebe…(dein, -e, -en)

I can never get enough…!
Von…kriege ich nie genug!

Let me take a picture of your…!
Lass mich ein Foto von dein- (-em,-er, -en)…knipsen!

Can I shave your…?
Kann ich dein- (-e, -en)…rasieren?

> **Pussy**
> *Muschi (f)/Maus (f)*
>
> **Cunt**
> *Fotze (f)/Möse (f)*
>
> **Hairy pussy**
> *Fellfrosch (m)*
> Literally, "furry frog"
>
> **Shaved pussy**
> *Schoßglatze (f)*

Pussy hawk
Irokese (m)
Literally, the "Iroquois Mohawk"

Clit
Perle (f)

Pussy lips
Schamlappen (f)
A play on the non-vulgar *Schamlippen*. Here it means "shame rags."

Tight pussy
Knackmumu (f)

Cameltoe
Cameltoe (n)

Pussy juice
Mösensaft (m)

Cock
Schwanz (m)

Johnson
Lümmel (m)

Dick
Puller (m)/Hammer (m)

Wiener
Wurst (f)

Pecker
Pimmel (m)

Pork sword
Fleischlanze (f)

Trouser snake
Aal (m)

Hard-on
Ständer (m)/
Latte (f)

Head
Helm (m)/Haube
(f)
Literally, "helmet"

THE SAUSAGE TRAY)))
DIE WURSTPLATTE

Like the selection of sausages available in a German deli, the variety of names for a man's best friend is just as diverse:

huge cock	*Oschi (pl)/Riesenschwanz (pl)*
hung like a horse	*Pferdeschwanz (pl)* [literally, "ponytail"]
tiny dick	*Pimmelchen (pl)*
limp dick	*Schlapschwanz (pl)/Schlapnudel (pl)*
big dick	*Fleischpeitsche (pl)* [literally, "flesh whip"]/ *dicke Wurst (pl)/Bockwurst (pl)*
shriveled dick	*KaWaMiPi* [short for *Kalt Wasser Mini Pimmel*—"cold water dick"]

The rim of the head
Eichelkranz (m)
Literally, "crown of the acorn"

Foreskin
Kragen (m) /Bananenschale (f)
Literally, "collar" and "banana peel"

Dick cheese
Nillenkäse (m)

Nuts
Nüsse (pl)

Nads
Klöten (pl)

Balls
Eier (pl)

Ball sack
Sack (m)

Pubes
Schamhaar (n)

Shaved pubes
Pimmelfriseur (m)

·····Tits and ass
Möpse und Kiste

Can I touch your…?
Kann ich dein- (-e, -en)…anfassen?

Can I suck on your…?
Kann ich an dein- (-e, -en)…lutschen?

Can I spank your…?
Kann ich dein- (-e, -en)…knallen?

Can I fuck your…?
Kann ich dein- (-e, -en)…ficken?

> **tits**
> *Titten (f)*
>
> **hooters**
> *Hupen (f)*
> Literally, "honkers"
>
> **jugs**
> *Dinger (f)*
>
> **puppies**
> *Möpse (f)*
>
> **nipples**
> *Schnuller (f)*
> Literally, "pacifier"
>
> **nips**
> *Nippel (f)*
>
> **erect nipples**
> *Igelnasen (f)*
> Literally, "hedgehog noses"
>
> **nipple ring**
> *Nippelknochen (m)*
>
> **ass**
> *Arsch (m)*
>
> **ass crack**
> *Po-Rille (f)*

BOOBS)))
DIE MOLKEREI

All breasts are beautiful, from A to DDD.

mosquito bites	*Mückenstiche [pl]*
breastless	*Flachland [n]*
flat-chested	*Bügelbrett [n]*
barely-breasted	*BMW (Brett mit Warzen) [literally, "a board with nipples"]*
medium-breasted	*pralle Titten [pl] [plump ... but not too big]*
well-endowed	*viel Holz vor der Hütte haben [literally, "a lot of wood in front of the cabin"]*
big tits	*dicke Hupen*
"Dolly Parton" tits	*Dickmanns [pl] [refers to a marshmallow candy that resembles large breasts]*
beautiful tits	*Porschetitten [pl] [the sportscar of tits]*
fake tits	*Kunsttitten [pl]/Silikonbrüste [pl]*

asshole
Rosette (f)

hairy asshole
Afterbart (m)

anus
Anus (m)

the 'taint
Damm (m)

·····Sex acts
Geschlechtsverkehr

Wanna try…?
Willst du mal…ausprobieren?

I like…
Ich stehe auf…

I'm tired of…
Ich habe genug von…

...is boring.
...ist langweilig.

...gets me hot.
...macht mich heiß.

...turns me on.
...macht mich an.

> **Kissing**
> *Knutschen*
>
> **To suck**
> *Saugen /Lutschen*
>
> **Cuddling**
> *Kuscheln*
>
> **Dry humping**
> *Petting*
>
> **Finger banging**
> *Fingerficken*
>
> **Cunnilingus**
> *Muschilecken/Fotzenlecken*
>
> **Fellatio**
> *Blasen*
>
> **Playing the skin flute**
> *Flötensolo (f) (spielen)*
> Literally, "a flute solo"
>
> **Swallowing**
> *Schlücken*
>
> **Facial**
> *Ins Gesicht abspritzen/Sperma-Regen (m)*
> Literally, "sperm-rain"
>
> **Pearl necklace**
> *Schneebart (m)*
> Literally, "snow beard"
>
> **Face sitting**
> *Gesichtssitzen/Queening* (from English)

Sixty-nine
69-er or Neunundsechziger Stellung (f)

Titty fucking
Tittenficken

Missionary style
Bambi-sex

Doggy style
Hündchenstellung (f)

Woman on top
Frau-oben

Wanna give me head?
Willst du mir einen blasen?

·····Sexcessories
Fickzeuge

Because the only thing that should come between you and
your partner is a condom…or a strap-on dildo, or your best
friend's hot mom.

Do you have (a)…?
Hast Du mal (einen, eine, ein)…?

Let's try using (a)…
Lass uns mal (einen, eine, ein)…benutzten.

condom.
Gummi. (m)

sex toy.
Sex-spielzeug. (n)
(also the English
"sex-toy")

lube.
Gleitmittel. (n)

dildo.
Dildo. (m)

double dildo.
Doppeldildo. (m)

ass-beads.
Lustkugeln. (pl)

butt plug.
Po-stöpsel. (m)

strap-on.
Umschnaller. (m)

vibrator.
Vibrator. (m)

handcuffs.
Handschellen. (pl)

whip.
Peitsche. (f)

mask.
Maske. (f)

rubber suit.
Gummianzug. (m)

cigarette.
Kippe. (f)

enema.
Einlauf. (m)

Kink
Bizarres

Sure, the Japanese invented Bukkake and the Dutch got you into Zoophilia, but they ain't got nothing on German *Scheiße*-porn! German society is all about structure, order, and discipline. So it's not surprising that in their private lives a lot of Germans get into weird sex and crazy fetishes, like chowing down on their lover's shit, for instance. Berlin, Cologne, Hamburg, and Vienna all have huge networks of fetish clubs, swinger bars, and brothels. Berlin's long-standing swinger club *Bar Möchtegern* is always free for the ladies and you get free drinks on the weekends. Go there to watch some guy get spanked with a Bible while you find someone to pee on. Here are a few terms to help you fulfill all your sick-ass dreams.

Be gentle with me!
Sei sanft mit mir!

Be rough with me!
Sei hart mit mir!

Be strict with me!
Sei streng mit mir!

Fuck my brains out!
Fick mich durch!

Whip me!
Peitsch mich aus!

Fuck me!
Fick mich!

I'm into…
Ich steh auf…

Let's try…
Lass uns mal…austesten?

> **rough sex.**
> *harten Sex.*
>
> **threesome.**
> *Dreier.*
>
> **group sex.**
> *Rudelbumsen.*
>
> **bisexual sex.**
> *Bi-sex.*
>
> **bondage.**
> *Fesselspiele. (pl)*

S&M.
Sado-Maso Spiele. (pl)

wax play.
Wachsspiele. (pl)
The suffix "*-spiele*" can be added to your favorite perversion to create a whole new lexicon of kink.

Boarding School Sex.
Internatssex. (m)
Germans are almost as excited about sex scenarios surrounding discipline and punishment in boarding schools as they are about beer and soccer.

anal sex.
Po-Sex. (m)

red wings.
Rotbart. (m)

female ejaculation.
Mösensprudel. (m)

scat.
Naturkaviar. (n)
Literally, "nature's caviar"

fisting.
Faustficken.

golden shower.
Pissspiele. (pl)/...Wassersport. (m)

golden shower.
jemanden anpinkeln. (to give)*/...sich anpinkeln lassen.* (to receive)

piss drinking.
Natursekt trinken.

tongue bath.
Zungenbad. (n)

vomit sex./Roman Shower.
Römern.
Literally, "to do the Roman." *Römern* is a versatile verb meaning anything from scat and watersports, to erotic vomiting and just plain fucking. Basically anything that is sexually deviant can be considered *Römern*.

•••••I'm coming
Mir Kommt's

Lucky for you, "to cum" is spelled and conjugated the same
way as "to come," because the last thing you want to think
of during the throes of passion is whether your conjugation
is correct. The only thing that might throw you off is the old
two-way preposition issue (*in* and *auf*), but hey, who's going to
correct your grammar when you're fucking like rabbits?

Can you get it up?
Kannst du einen hoch kriegen?

I've got a boner.
Ich habe einen Ständer.

Oww! That hurts.
Aua! Das tut weh.

This feels really good.
Das fühlt sich geil an.

I'm starting to get off.
Das geilt mich auf.

I'm about to come.
Mir kommt's.

DO IT...)))
MACH'S SCHON...

faster.	*schneller.*
slower.	*langsamer.*
harder.	*härter.*
softer.	*sanfter.*
more.	*weiter.*

Mmmm, I want to drink up your...!
Ich will dein-(-e, -en) ... abtrinken!

sperm	*Sperma (n)*
cum	*Ficksahne (f)* (literally, "fuck sauce")
jizz	*Pilzsauce (f)* (literally, "mushroom sauce")
twat sauce	*Fotzensaft (m)*
cream	*Schlagsahne (f)*

I'm coming!
Ich komme!

Where should I shoot it?
Wohin sollte ich es spritzen?

Come...
Spritz...

>**in my ass!**
>*in meinem Arsch!*

>**on my face!**
>*auf mein Gesicht!*

>**on my pussy!**
>*auf meine Muschi!*

>**on my tits!**
>*auf meine Titten!*

I just came.
Ich bin gerade gekommen.

Can you go again?
Kannst du noch einmal?

I'm gonna jizz!
Ich spritze gleich ab!

·····Getting to know you (sexually)

Germans aren't all blonde-haired, blue-eyed, Lederhosen-
and Dirndl-wearing caricatures from some Disney fairy tale.
Deep down inside many of them are sluts, pervs, man-whores,
and sex fiends just like you. So ditch the boring phrases from
those lame getting-to-know-you games you played in class
(no one gives a shit whether your favorite color is blue, or that
you *really* like pizza) and ask the questions that truly matter.

Are you (a)...?
Bist Du ein (-e, -en)...?

gay
Schwule (m)/schwul (adj.)

fag
Schwuchtel (m)

queen
Tunte (f)

lesbian
Lesbe (f)/lesbisch (adj.)

bisexual guy
Bi-Mann (m)/Bi-Jung

bisexual girl
Bi-Frau (f)/Bi-Mädel

slut
Schlampe (f) (male or female)

bitch
Zicke (f)

cheap fuck
Hobby-nutte (f)

lousy lay
Schlefi (m) (male or female)

whore
Hure (f)/Nutte (f)

town whore
Dorf-Matratze (f)
Literally, "village mattress"

"MOVIE NIGHT")))
DVD-ABEND

"Video nights" are popular among small groups of German friends: beer, food, friends, and a flick; what could be better? But when you take into account that *DVD-Abend* is also a euphemism for a sexy night at home, you may have to read between the lines the next time a "friend" invites you over for a movie night.

Hey baby, wanna make a video?
Na Schätzchen, wollen wir einen Heimporno drehen?

What? Are you nuts?
Spinnst du, oder was?

No, you just make me so fucking horny. Your tits are incredible.
Nee, du geilst mich einfach auf... Deine prallen Möpse sind mega scharf... echte Porschetitten.

Can you get it up?
Kannst du einen Hochkriegen?

Hell yeah, I'm already there. Let me see your pussy!
Na logo. Zeig mir doch deine Maus!

And I wanna see your pork sword!
Und du deine Fleischpeitsche!

I've got a surprise for your pussy hawk.
Ich habe eine Überraschung für deine Landebahn.

Holy shit! You shaved your balls!
Bhoa! Voll der Pimmelfriseur!

Ok, lick my nuts and give me some head!
Zuerst kannst du mir den Sack lecken und mir ein Kind abtrinken!

Hey, let's be nice now. Ladies first!
Nee, wer ficken will muss Freundlich sein. Zuerst must du aus der Pfanne essen!

girl who sleeps her way to the top
Abi-nutte (f)
"*Abitur*" is the equivalent of high school graduation, "*Abi*" is the abbreviation.

virgin
Jungfrau (f) (male or female)

Well then, let me finger you first. Your pussy is so tight. I'll make you squirt!
Eben, lass mich dich fingern. Deine Knackmumu ist geil. Dich bringe ich zum sprüdeln!

I'd rather have you tickle my asshole while you kiss my pussy lips!
Kitzel doch meinen Po, während du an meine Punzen knabberst!

Yeeeah! Then I'll fuck you silly!
Bhooooa! Dann werde ich dich auswuchten!

Maybe if you're a good boy, you can take my back door!
Wenn du brav bist, lass ich dich mein Mokkastübchen besuchen!

Get your butt plug!
Hol doch deinen Po-stöpsel!

I'd rather have the beads.
Der Luststab wäre mir lieber.

I'll get the handcuffs.
Ich hole meine Handschellen.

Are you gonna talk all night or fuck?
Willst du mich vollabern oder ficken?

Fuck, we're out of condoms!
Eh, Scheiße. Wir haben keinen Gummi!

How about you jerk off on my tits while I rub one out?
Wie wär's mit 'ner Perlenkette während ich die Trommel rühre?

Hey, we can still do some tittyfuckin' and I can eat you out. A little 69 couldn't hurt either!
Na also, Tittenficken und Muschilecken sind noch im Programm. Ein 69 kann nie schaden!

Sounds like a great night to stay in!
Das wird aber ein schöner DVD-Abend sein!

tranny
Transe (m)

M.I.L.F.
Milf (f)

bull-dyke
Kampflesbe (f)
Literally, "combat lesbian"

lipstick lesbian
"LiStiLe" (f) /Lippenstift Lesbe

dirty whore
Dreckshure (f)

call girl
Callgirl (f)/Escort (f)

player, pimp
Checker (m)/Poser (m)

two-pump chump
10-Sekunden-Tom (m)

horny person
geile Sau (f)

sadist
Sadist (m)

masochist
Masochist (m)

pervert
Perverser (m)

foot fetishist
Fuß-fetischist (m)

rubber fetishist
Gummi-fetischist (m)

voyeur/Peeping Tom
Spanner (m)

dominatrix
Domina (f)

dominator
Dominus (m)

CHAPTER 6

ANGRY GERMAN
BÖSES DEUTSCH

·····Enemies
Feinde

There are varying types of douche bags in this world, and knowing how to label and hate them accordingly is an important skill for any young misanthrope. The important thing is to find targets for your building aggression and bitch about them accordingly.

Neighbors
Nachbarn (pl)

> **My neighbors shoot porno movies on their balcony.**
> *Meine **Nachbarn** drehen auf ihrem Balkon Porno Filme.*

Landlord
Vermieter (m/f) (-in)

> **My landlord is in the Russian mob.**
> *Mein **Vermieter** ist voll der Russenmafiatyp.*

Boss
Chef (m/f) (-in)

> **My boss** is a fuckin' drunk.
> *Mein **Chef** ist voll der Säufer.*

Ex-girlfriend
Ex (f)

> **My ex-girlfriend** turned lesbo.
> *Meine **Ex** ist Lesbe geworden.*

Ex-boyfriend
Ex (m)

> **My ex-boyfriend** was making out with my brother!
> *Mein **Ex** hat mit meinem Bruder geknutscht!*

Mother-in-law
Schwiegermonster (n)
Literally, "monster-in-law"

My mother-in-law is completely schizo.
Mein Schwiegermonster ist echt durchgeknallt.

Peeping Tom
Spanner (m)

Some Peeping Tom was hanging out by your window yesterday.
Ein Spanner lungerte gestern vor deinem Fenster herum.

Deadbeat
Gammler (m)

Markus has owed me 100 Euros for months, what a deadbeat.
Markus schuldet mir seit Monaten 100 Euro, voll der Gammler.

Jocks
Sportler (m)

Jocks really piss me off!
Sportler nerven mich total!

Lawyers
Anwälte (pl)

Why are all lawyers so shitty?
Wieso sind alle Anwälte so fies?

Politicians
Politiker (pl)

Are German politicians crooked too?
Sind deutsche Politker auch so korrupt?

Cops
Bullen (pl)

German cops don't really look intimidating.
Die deutschen Bullen sehen gar nicht so gefährlich aus.

·····Talkin' shit
Scheiße reden

When was the last time you went on for hours talking about what a nice person so-and-so is? Umm…probably never. For some strange reason, humans just universally prefer to talk shit about each other. Why? Because humans are petty, that's why. So why not join the gossip-mongering fray by making fun of all the petty assholes out there?

Man, I can't stand those two.
*Alda, die Beiden kann ich **nicht aushalten**.*

What a complete asshole.
*Was für ein **Arschloch**.*

What a dumb-ass!
*Voll der **Depp**!*

He is full of shit!
*Er hat nur **Luft im Sack**!*
Literally, "he has air in his balls"

She is always talking shit about us.
*Sie **redet nur Scheiße** über uns.*

Whoa, she's fuckin' disgusting.
*Bhoa, ist die voll **eklig**.*

She is a stuck-up bitch.
*Sie ist 'ne **hochnäsige Zicke**.*

He thinks he's so cool.
*Er hält sich für was **Besonderes**.*

What a fucking traitor!
*Was für ein **Verräter**!*

You should see his MySpace page. Totally creepy.
*Du solltest sein MySpaceprofil sehen, echt **unheimlich**.*

That guy Holger makes me a little nervous.
*Der Holger macht mich etwas **nervös**.*

Stefanie's a total kiss ass.
*Stefanie spielt heute wieder **die Analraupe**.*
Literally, "acting like an anal caterpillar"

Watch out for him, he'll totally fuck you over!
*Pass mal auf, der **lässt dich voll im Stich**!*

Don't let him fool you, he's just blowin' smoke up yer ass!
*Lass ihn dich nicht täuschen, der **bläst dir nur Puderzucker in den Arsch**!*
Literally, "blowing powdered sugar in your ass"

They used to be best friends until she found out the other one was a total slut.
*Die waren doch super befreundet, bis die eine es mitbekommen hat, dass die andere 'ne **miese Bumskuh** ist.*

She'll never be able to make it up to me.
*Die kann's mir nie **wieder gutmachen**.*

Fuck her!/She can go fuck herself!
Sie kann sich verpissen!

He's a total chump!
*Er ist Voll die **Luftpumpe**!*

She's just a little cry-baby.
*Sie ist echt nur ein **Tränentier**.*

THE HANDY DANDY LIST OF COMMON INSULTS)))
BELEIDIGUNGEN UND IHRE HANDHABUNG

Fucker
Penner (m) [literally, "a bum," but you can also just call a guy a fucker and it carries the same weight.]

Asshole
Arschloch (n)

Bitch
Zicke (f)

Sissy/Wussy
Luscher (m) [Really a sucker, but the same insult as a wussy. *Waschlappen (m)* is also a close second and means "dishrag."]

Son of a bitch
Arschmade (f) [literally, "ass-maggot"]

Cunt
Fotze (f)

Slut
Schlampe (f)

Whore
Hure (f)

Cocksucker
Schwunzlatscher (m) [Pun on the literal translation "*Schwanzlutscher*." It comes off funnier and more insulting.]

Motherfucker
Motherfucker (m) [This is a real gem. I laughed at the first guy who called me this, cuz it sounded like "muzza-fucka." He wasn't amused.]

Piece of shit
Scheißkerl (m)

Shithead
Drecksau (f) [literally, "a dirty pig"]

Butt-pirate
Popirat (m)

·····Gettin' pissed
Sauer werden

Everybody's got their own threshold when it comes to containing their anger. Push them over it and they'll quickly lose their cool. Luckily, most Germans will tell you that you're pushing their buttons before they open a can of Teutonic whoop-ass on you. Here are some helpful words you'll need to let people know that you're starting to get pissed.

Stupid tourists...
Dumme Touristen...

Just about everything...
Fast alles...

The way he/she looks...
Wie er/sie aussieht...

The way he/she talks...
Wie er/sie spricht...

His/her attitude...
Seine/ihre Haltung...

>**bugs the hell outta me.**
>*stört mich total.*
>
>**makes my skin crawl.**
>*geht mir unter die Haut.*
>
>**drives me crazy!**
>*macht mich verrückt!*
>
>**is really annoying.**
>*ist voll nervig.*
>
>**pisses me off.**
>*pisst mich an.*
>
>**makes me wanna puke.**
>*ist zum Kotzen.*

gets my shorts in a knot.
raubt mir den letzten Nerven.

You're really bustin' my balls!
Du gehst mir auf den Sack!

·····Goin' postal
Durchdrehen

German is full of words for going nuts and losing your shit. Maybe it's the crappy winter weather. Maybe it's cuz they're surrounded by nine other countries that blame them for two world wars. Sometimes I think the only thing preventing Germans from going completely insane is that they've got great beer and get four weeks of paid vacation a year. Whatever it is, Germans are more likely to express their insanity or anger in less violent ways than shooting up a post office.

To lose it
Abdrehen

> **He spilled his beer on my new shoes and I lost it.**
> *Der hat Bier auf meine neuen Schuhe gekippt und ich bin einfach **abgedreht**.*

To go postal
Durchdrehen

> **When my girlfriend finds out that we're screwing, she's gonna go postal.**
> *Wenn meine Freundin es mitkriegt, dass wir bumsen, wird sie **durchdrehen**.*

To flip out
Ausflippen

> **I can't handle it anymore, I'm about to flip out.**
> *Ich kann's nicht mehr ertragen, ich **flippe gleich aus**.*

To lose your grip
Abticken

> **Dude, get a grip.**
> *Äh man, **tick nicht ab**.*

To be nuts
Spinnen

> **Are you fucking nuts?**
> ***Spinnst du** oder was?*

Totally mental
Am Blitz geleckt haben
Literally, "to lick a lightning bolt"

> **That guy's totally mental!**
> *Der hat wohl am **Blitz geleckt**!*

The shit has hit the fan.
Nun ist die Kacke am Dampfen.

·····Fighting
Kämpfen

Germany is pretty peaceful these days. The fallout from that whole WWI-and-II thing kinda put the kibosh on German displays of aggression. But just because they aren't going to invade France anytime soon, doesn't mean that there's no violence in the country. Though you don't really have to worry about UK-style soccer riots or L.A.-style drive-by shootings, politics can still get pretty heated. And if you get caught in the middle of a standoff between converging groups of left-wing punks and right-wing skins, watch for bricks aimed at your head.

> **Gotta problem?**
> *Ist was?*

THE CHUCK NORRIS DICTIONARY)))
DAS CHUCK NORRIS KAMPFLEXICON

Punch	Schlag (m)
Kick	Tritt (m)
Karate chop	Karateschlag (m)
Roundhouse kick	Breitseite (f)
Choke hold	Würgegriff (m)
Uppercut	Uppercut (m)
Slap	Klaps (m)
Backhand	Rückhandschlag (m)
Headlock	Schwitzkasten (m) (literally, "the sweat box")
Sucker punch	Suckerpunch (m)
Haymaker	Schwinger (m)

What about it?
Na und?

What's up with that shit?
Was soll der Scheiß?

Whatcha want, dipshit?
*Was willste, du **Pappnase**?*

I hate you.
Dich hasse ich.

Kiss my ass!
Leck mich doch am Arsch!

Piss off!
Verpiss dich!

Ok, playtime's over.
Schluss mit lustig.

Go fuck yourself!
Fick dich ins Knie!
Literally, "go fuck yourself in the knee"

Asshole!
Arschloch!

Hey, jerk-off!
*Na, du **Wichser**!*

Shut your trap.
Halt die Klappe.

Shut the fuck up!
Halt's Maul!

I don't give a shit!
Ist mir doch scheißegal!

You worthless piece of shit!
Du mieses Stück Scheiße!

Want me to rearrange your face?
Sollte ich dir die Fresse polieren?
Literally, "polish your snout"

Beat it.
Geh kacken.
Literally, "go take a shit"

What, you chicken?
Wat, haste' Schiss?

Pussy!
Weichei!

Bring it on!
Na mach schon!

·····Avoiding violence
Gewalt vermeiden

German beat-downs are pretty rare. Most of the fights you'll encounter in Germany will be between two drunk guys and last all of about thirty seconds. But if you do happen to find yourself in a sticky situation, try out the following verbal gems to cool down some hotheads, break up a fight or save yourself from getting stomped on.

Take it easy, man.
Eh man, locker bleiben.

Just take a deep breath.
Einfach tief einatmen.

Stop it.
Schluss damit.

Enough with the "tough guy" act.
Sei doch nicht so macho, eh.

Violence ain't the answer.
Gewalt ist keine Lösung.

It really ain't that big a deal, is it?
Ist alles doch pipifax, oder?

Dude, keep your shit together.
Mensch, reiß dich zusammen.

Bro, forget it.
Vergiss es, Digga.

This is really childish bullshit.
Das ist ja Kinderkacke.

Actually I'm a pacifist.
Eigentlich bin ich Pazifist.

Hey, cut that shit out.
Hey, hör auf mit dem Scheiß.

I'd rather not get involved.
Ich misch mich lieber nicht ein.

Fuck this, I'm callin' the cops.
Scheiß drauf, ich hol' die Bullen.

·····The cops
die Bullen

As the son of a retired sheriff, I have nothing but respect for police. But German cops are kind of a joke. They don't do much except hang around shopping centers, drive around in VW Golf and Passat cop cars, and look bored. If it weren't for the guns, they'd almost look like they were going to pick their kids up from soccer practice. The filth in Bavaria can be real dicks, though. My girlfriend once got stopped in a park in Munich because she was using a mirror to check her contact lens. Munich's finest thought she was sniffing coke and went on a whole "not in my town, blah, blah, blah" rant.

Riot cops are another story. They stand guard at all the political demonstrations, train stations, and soccer matches, and they just wait for an excuse to run you over in their "green and white party bus" or hose you down with water cannons.

Fuckin' cops.
Scheiß Bullen.

Here come the...
Hier kommt /kommen...

police.
Polizei. (f)

popo.
Polente. (f)

pigs.
Bullen. (pl)

occifer.
Pozelei. (f)
A pun on *Polizei*. Like saying "Howdy Occifer!"

fuzz.
Buletten. (f)

That jerk's an undercover cop.
*Der Spacken da ist 'n **Zivilbulle**.*

The Paddy Wagon's comin'.
*Der **Grün-weiße Party Bus** kommt.*
Most cop cars are green and white and so is the bus they haul your ass away in.

Put that shit away.
Weg mit dem Scheiß.

Dude, let's bail.
*Eh, **lass uns abhauen**.*

Don't say shit.
Schnauze.
Literally, "snout"

Dude, don't snitch.
*Hey Digga, nicht **verpfeifen**.*

They'll throw your ass in the clink for that.
*Dafür kommste in den **Knast**.*

If you're brave enough to taunt the pigs with your new anarchist friends, try out the following German classics. But be careful, cuz German cops can throw your ass in jail just for making fun of them. The crime is called *Amtsbeleidigung* (insulting the officer) and can land you in the clink. Seriously.

Ficken Bullen nicht Kühe?
Don't bulls fuck cows? (This is kinda like asking "Do you smell bacon?" in front of a cop.)

A.C.A.B./F.D.P.
All Cops Are Bastards/Fuck da' Police (both are favorite chants at riots and demonstrations)

CHAPTER 7

POPPY GERMAN
POP DEUTSCH

Unlike in France, where 40 percent of music played on radio stations has to be French, Germany doesn't have a bunch of laws that try to protect their cultural heritage. As a result, American pop culture has really started to muscle in on everyday German life. Some people hate it, some people love it, but it appears to be here to stay. So don't be surprised when you flip on the TV to catch Mr. T pitying the fool in German on *Das A-Team*.

•••••Music
Mucke

Are you into...?
Stehst du auf...?

What's the deal with...?
Was ist es eigentlich mit...?

I wanna hear some...
Ich will etwas...hören.

...is totally awesome.

ist echt der Hammer.

Literally, "the hammer"

...is for kids.

ist für den Kindergarten.

...is kinda gay.

ist etwas schwul.

Pop

Just as mainstream and vanilla as it is in English. Although Germany has its own pop groups, they usually sing in English. *No Angels, LaFee,* and *Monrose* are chick groups that especially suck. Girls love them, though, so you might have to pretend to like them.

Rock and Roll

No matter where you go, rock is rock.

Krautrock

Weird psychedelic progressive rock that got popular in the '60s and '70s in West Germany. *Can, Tangerine Dream,* and *Wallenstein* are three *Krautrock* groups still big with stoners.

Ostrock

East Germany's answer to *Krautrock*, but not exclusively for hippies.

Punk

Everything from really hard-core political punk like *Dritte Wahl* and *Slime* to fun, party punk like *Die Ärtzte* and the original German party punks *Die Toten Hosen*.

Boy Groups

Although American groups dominate this category (which is nothing to be proud of), Germans are taking over with the recent suck-cess of Tokio Hotel. Imagine if N'Sync and a Japanese pop band had creepy sex... this would be their kid.

Schlager

Originated as jazz-like film music in the '20s and '30s but stopped being cool in the '60s. It doesn't even sound good when you're drunk. Except for *Heino*, a

109

one-man, guitar-playing demon. He looks like a wall-eyed blonde version of Roy Orbison and sounds like Pat Boone with a big set of balls. Heino's the shit.

Volksmusik
Literally "the music of the people," it consists of traditional German music like the *Oompah* brass bands at Oktoberfest, or a crappy, modern-day synthesized version thereof. It's mostly ballads about the forest and mountains. *Omas* and *Opas* love this shit.

Rap/Hip-hop
American rappers are popular, but Hamburg and Berlin are the capitols of German hip-hop, with dozens of big-name rappers. *Die Fantastischen Vier* are like the German Beastie Boys.

Black Music
As you might guess, this is pretty much music by black people. The charts cover R&B and soul as well as reggae. The name isn't meant to be derogatory.

Dark Wave
A favorite of German Goth kids, extra spooky and extra fruity.

Industrial
Einstürzende Neubauten are the godfathers of industrial music, which is fitting, seeing that their name

translates to "collapsing new buildings." No one else can make a power saw sound like sweet music quite the way these guys do.

Electronic
Kraftwerk were the original pioneers of German electronic music, but the genre has since expanded to include everything from house to experimental to techno. There are a lot of good German electronic bands and a lot of shitty ones, too. *Le Rok* is one of the awesome ones. Check them out.

Neue deutsche Welle (NDW)
Meaning "New German Wave." Remember *Falco* and *Nena*? *NDW* is '80s music that made it cool again for bands to sing in German. Like British New Wave, there are both "underground" and "pop" versions in Germany too. All of it still kicks ass and is still pretty popular in clubs. Chicks dig it if you get out and dance whenever someone spins *99 Luftballoons*.

Hamburger Schule
Meaning the "Hamburg School." German indie rock comes from all over the country but is especially synonymous with Hamburg, similar to the way that grunge was synonymous with Seattle back in the '90s. *Die Goldenen Zitronen*, *Blumfeld*, and *Tocotronic* are a few Hamburg School bands that rock the *Kiez*.

"Neue" neue deutsche Welle
Bands like *Spillsbury*, *Tomte*, and *Kettcar* are the "new" New German Wave. Take the best of *Hamburger Schule* and *NDW* and you've got something equivalent to retro-'80s music with German lyrics.

Neue deutsche Härte "New German Hardness" *Rammstein* introduced the U.S. to the genre. It's also referred to as *Tanzmetall* or "dance metal," which is, well, metal you can dance to.

I only **sing in the shower.**
*Ich **singe nur unter der Dusche**.*

Do you have a favorite German band?
Hast du eine deutsche Lieblingsband?

What groups do you like?
Welche Gruppen magst du?

Who's your favorite singer?
Wer ist dein Lieblingsänger?

Do you play an instrument?
Spielst du ein Instrument?

Stage diving is still cool.
Stagediving ist immer noch cool.

·····TV and movies
Film und Fernsehen

Germans are bombarded with tons of dubbed American TV shows and movies. It's kinda funny at first, but then really sad, because you realize that the same voiceover actor who does John Travolta also does Bruce Lee. WTF?

Do you guys ever watch German shows?
Schaut ihr keine deutschen Sendungen?

Let's watch...
Gucken wir...

...is the best show on TV.
...ist die geilste Sendung.

Big Brother
Yeah, Germany has a version of this show too. The only thing that makes it remotely cooler than the U.S. version is that it can show nudity. Nothing beats spying on naked people on CCTV.

LOST IN TRANSLATION)))

Germans love American movies, but *Be Kind Rewind* doesn't exactly move the masses in *Deutschland*. As such, German distributors feel the need to translate film titles to make them more appealing to the average German moviegoer. Fortunately for us, this makes for some seriously funny shit. Some of the revamped titles are so bad they make *Snakes on a Plane* seem inspired.

Beverly Hills Ninja
Die Kampfwurst [The Combat Sausage]

In Bruges
Brügge sehen...und sterben? [See Bruges ... and Die?]

Ferris Bueller's Day Off
Ferris macht blau [Ferris Fakes Being Sick]

Fast Times at Ridgemont High
Ich glaub ich stehe im Wald [I Think I'm Standing in the Woods]

Bill & Ted's Excellent Adventure
Bill & Teds verrückte Reise durch die Zeit [Bill and Ted's Crazy Adventure Through Time]

Stripes
Ich glaub', mich knutscht ein Elch! [I Think a Moose is Kissing Me!]

Deutschland Sucht den Superstar (DSDS)

The Germanic version of *American Idol*. The contestants here are just as "talented" as they are in America.

Tatort

The classic German cop show that just about everyone watches, even if they don't admit it. *CSI* is for chumps; it's all about *Tatort*.

Lindenstraße

This soap opera or *Telenovelle* about a bunch of neighbors living in Munich has been on since the Cold War. It's set in Munich, but is actually filmed in Köln. The show set off an uproar in 1990 when it showed gays kissing for the first time on prime-time German TV.

Schlag den Raab
A challenger competes against Stefan Raab (a German Tom Green) for a million Euros. Kinda like a Japanese game show, but less hokey.

Richterin Barbara Salesch
The German Judge Judy is less of a bitch but still has red hair and annoys everyone who doesn't adore her. There are like ten different German court TV shows, all of which provide not only a frightening look into the underbelly of German society, but are good for a laugh too.

Pastewka
The best German sitcom about nothing. Jerry Seinfeld would be Pastewka if he were chubbier, German, and funnier than his cast mates.

·····Humor
Humor

Like British cuisine or French military, German humor sounds like a contradiction. Nothing could be further from the truth. Germans are hilarious. Their diverse regional customs and dialects make for a lot of cultural misunderstandings and thus, serious comedic fodder. German comics capitalize on this, making fun of everybody around, and usually in their local dialect. It's kinda like Larry the Cable Guy drawling "Get'er done" in his Southern twang, except, you know, funny.

Schadenfreude (f)
Who else but the Germans could have a term that translates as "malicious joy." This is all about laughing at the pain and misfortune of others.

Jokes
Witze (pl)
Witz means "joke," but if you stick *witz* at the end of your favorite subject you've just invented a whole new genre of jokes.

Hey, you know any...?
Sag mal, kennste einige...?

All right, enough of the stupid...
Also, die blöden...reichen mir schon.

...are the funniest.
...sind voll lustig.

White trash jokes
Prollwitze
For some reason these are universally funny, unless you're a *Proll*.

> ***Wie lange bleibt ein Proll-mädel Jungfrau?***
> ***-Solange sie schneller läuft als ihre Brüder!***
> How long does a *Proll* girl remain a virgin?
> -As long as she can still outrun her brothers!

Bureaucrat jokes
Beamtenwitze
Lots of Germans think their bureaucrats are lazy pains in the ass, so the masses fight back with humor.

> ***Treffen sich zwei Beamte im Flur. Der eine zum Anderen: "Na, kannst Du auch nicht schlafen?"***
> Two bureaucrats meet in the office hallway. One says to the other: "Can't sleep either?"

Soldier jokes
Soldatenwitze
All German males 18 and older have to join the army. Laughter (and lots of drinking) help them get through their service.

> ***"Sagen Sie, Herr Gefreiter Müller, haben Sie beim Bund eigentlich noch eine eigene Meinung?"***
> ***"Da muß ich erst meinen Spieß fragen!"***
> "Say, Private Müller, do you still think for yourself in the army?"
> "I don't know, I gotta ask my Sergeant!"

REGIONAL JOKES)))
REGIONALWITZE

Germany's major cultural and linguistic dividing line is north/south, but the old border between the former east and west is still a cultural barrier for some, making for some serious comedic warfare.

NORTHWEST GERMAN JOKES
OSTFRIESENWITZE

Ostfriesland is in Northwest Germany and has lots of farms. For some reason *Ostfriesland* has gotten a bad rap and is the butt of a lot of jokes, kinda like Poland back in the day.

> *Wie versenkt man ein ostfriesisches U-Boot?*
> *-Anklopfen!*
> How do you sink an *East-Friesian* submarine?
> -Knock on the door!

EAST GERMAN JOKES
OSSIWITZE

Ex-East Germans (*Ossis*) are still the targets of jokes by western Germans even 20 years after unification.

> *Ein Grenzsoldat an der Berliner Mauer zum anderen:*
> *- "Was hältst du von der DDR?"*
> *"Dasselbe wie du."*
> *- "Dann muss ich dich verhaften."*
> Two border guards are on the Berlin Wall, the one says to the other:
> -"Whattya think of the DDR?"
> "Same as you."
> -"Well then I've got to arrest you."

WEST GERMAN JOKES
WESSIWITZE

Tired of the bad rap by western Germans (*Wessis*), *Ossis* fire back with jabs of their own.

> *Was erhält man wenn man einen Ossi mit einem Wessi kreuzt?*
> *-Einen arroganten Arbeitslosen!*
> What do you get when you cross an *Ossi* and a *Wessi*?
> -An unemployed asshole!

BAVARIAN JOKES
BAYERNWITZE

Stereotypical Bavarians are fat, talk funny, and drink lots of beer. In other words: perfect joke material.

> *Was ist der Unterschied zwischen Türken und Bayern?*
> *-Türken sprechen meist besser Deutsch.*
> What's the difference between Turks and Bavarians?
> -Turks speak better German.

Cop jokes
Polizeiwitze
Cop jokes are great, especially when the pigs can't hear 'em.

> ***Was sind die vier schwersten Jahre im Leben eines Polizisten?***
> ***-Die erste Klasse.***
> What are the hardest four years in a cop's life?
> -The first grade.

Puns
Wortspiele (pl)
German is full of puns and they get tossed around like pretzels at Oktoberfest, like this classic:

> ***Aus Hackepeter wird Kacke später.***
> Out of ground beef will later be crap.

Hey, have you guys heard this one yet?
Na, habt ihr diesen schon gehört?

Was that meant to be funny?
Sollte das ein Witz sein?

Is there a punchline?
Gibt's 'ne Pointe?

You're a real retard, aren't you?
Du bist 'n echter Behindi, oder?

I laughed **my ass off**.
*Ich habe mich **totgelacht**.*

He's making a total **ass of himself**.
*Der **spielt den Affen**.*

·····German comedy acts
Deutsche Komiker

Loriot
Loriot is the absolute giant of classic German comedy. His sketches and cartoons exploit Schadenfreude to its fullest. Some think of him as Germany's answer to Monty Python, but he's way cooler cuz he's actually a real person.

Harald Schmidt
Germany's version of Letterman or Leno. Got some serious laughs (and shit) by poking fun at Hitler on national television.

Stefan Raab
He's the highbrow, lowbrow humor host of *TV Total* and just about anything else that's funny in Germany. He can seem kinda dickish, but really he just shows stupid people being stupid. His sidekick Elton used to play doorbell bingo and wake people up in the middle of the night to win prizes.

Elton Vs. Simon
Elton teamed up with friend Simon to bring German TV its own version of *Kenny Vs. Spenny*. But they one-upped the Canucks by evolving into a live show. What could be better than a live contest to see who can watch a porno the longest without sporting wood? Nothing, the answer is nothing.

Studio Braun
Hamburg's answer to the *Jerky Boys*. If you think prank calls that involve a guy getting raped by Sasquatch are hilarious, then you'll love this show.

Bully
A stand-up and sketch comedian from Munich who got huge with his TV show *Bullyparade* where he makes fun of

all things Bavarian and creates classic comedy sketches like his gay *Star Trek* and a Germanic version of the *Love Boat*.

Ausbilder Schmidt

Is he a comic or a drill sergeant? *Ausbuilder Schmidt* makes Triumph the insult comic dog look like that gay little Chihuahua from those Taco Bell commercials. I'm not sure if my side hurts from all the laughing or the sit-ups he made me do.

Atze Schröder

Germany's answer to Andrew Dice Clay is not as sexist or dumb and is like a thousand times funnier. Atze is a lovable, womanizing kiosk owner from the heart of industrial Germany, the *Ruhrpott*, and is the real blue-collar deal. Instead of rocking the leather jacket and pompadour, Schröder sports a cheesy perm and porno shades. Nobody knows his real identity.

FAMOUS GERMAN COMEDY QUOTES

"Evenin', Ding Dong Bingo's here, you could win 250 Euros!"
"N'abend, Bimmel Bingo ist hier, Sie können 250 Euro gewinnen!" (Elton)

"Fresh asparagus tea! And it's still hot!"
"Frischer Spargeltee! Der ist ja noch ganz heiß!" (Bullyparade)

"Mornin', you pussies!"
"Morgen, ihr Luschen!" (Ausbilder Schmidt)

"Yeah, yeah, I got it!"
"Ja nee, iss klar!" (Atze Schröder)

"Dickie wants to recite a Christmas poem for us!"----"Lickity split, chicken shit!"
"Dickie will uns jetzt ein Weihnachtsgedicht aufsagen!---zicke zacke Hühnerkacke!" (Loriot)

·····Fashion
Mode

When it comes to German fashion, most people think of guys in funny hats wearing socks with sandals. Nothing could be further from the truth. Berlin and Düsseldorf are major European fashion centers, and younger Germans, especially in the bigger cities, are always up on the latest styles and love anything new and different from the States. The old Cold War myth about Germans selling a kidney for a pair of blue jeans died out with online shopping. But you'll still make some new friends by trading your Abercrombie T-shirt for some weird-ass Euro shoes.

Fashion
Mode (f)

The "scene"
Szene (f)

Clothes
Klamotten (pl)

I'm into chicks/dudes who dress...
Ich stehe auf Mädchen/Typen, die...Klamotten tragen.

I only wear...clothes.
Ich trage nur...Klamotten

I'm totally...
Ich bin voll...

Sporty
Sportlich
Like you just came from the gym, but all stylish and put together, not gross and sweaty.

Preppy
Edel
Usually white sneakers, insanely expensive jeans, and Polo shirts.

Business
Amtlich/Business
For some reason all German businessmen have these weird blue dress shirts that they wear with everything.

Punk/Emo
Punk/Emo
Kinda like Hot Topic pop-punk style. These are the cute punkers you wanna take home.

Squatter/Crust-core
Anarcho-punk
More of a lifestyle than just fashion, these are the crust-core, peace punk kids who beg for change at train stations and let their dog piss on your leg.

Hipster/Indie rock
Indie
Skinny, pale dudes in track jackets with tight T-shirts, corduroy jeans, and old Adidas sneakers are the standard. For some reason German indie kids aren't as annoying as American ones.

Rockabilly
Oldschool
Basically rockabilly chicks and greaser dudes, but without the redneck vibe you get at a Mike Ness show. Lots of jeans and black T-shirts and tattoos. Like in the States, it's really popular with older punkers who don't wanna grow up.

Goth
Gothic
The standard uniform of the *Grufti* and Dark Wave crowd. They can run the spectrum from hot chicks with coffin purses to fruity dudes who look like the walking dead, ready to eat your soul.

Skinhead
Skin/Oi
A skinhead's trademark look is Fred Perry and Ben Sherman clothes with boots, suspenders, jeans, and, of course, a shaved head. Like in the States, most *Oi* kids aren't racist (these days skinhead doesn't automatically mean racist; it's just an anti-establishment attitude and style) and are usually pretty cool. But be on the lookout, cuz there are still some right-wing skins in Germany who might want to kick your ass for no reason.

Vintage
Second-hand/Vintage
Not crap from the Salvation Army, but actually good vintage threads. If you think your shitty Members Only jacket is cool, the average German *Secondhandladen* (vintage store) will blow you away. *Schrader* is a bitchin' store that sells vintage threads by the kilo, literally.

Mainstream
Streetwear
This is the generic term for youth fashions. Lots of American influence and pretty boring to look at.

Skater
Skater
As mainstream as this style's become, you may be surprised when you see a skater kid who actually owns and rides a skateboard. But in just about every German city there are still tons of skaters who brave the cobblestone streets with their boards and €90 Vans "Old Schools."

Hip-hop
Hiphop
These guys follow the trends in America, but it might take a while for Lil John's pimp cups to catch on.

Raver
Techno/Raver
Not just shitty music, but crappy fashion too. You can spot their rubber pants, pink hair, platform shoes, space-age backpacks, and ridiculous goggles

from across the train station. They look like anime characters who just huffed a bunch of Xanax.

Your outfit looks really…
Dein Outfit ist echt…

> **cute.**
> *hübsch.*

> **pretty.**
> *schön.*

> **stylish.**
> *modisch.*

> **expensive.**
> *teuer.*

> **cheap.**
> *billig.*

> **stupid.**
> *blöd.*

> **retarded.**
> *bescheuert.*

> **cheesy.**
> *kitschig.*

He/She's…
Er/Sie ist…

> **kinda tan.**
> *etwas gebräunt.*

> **kinda pale.**
> *etwas blass.*

> **hip.**
> *im Trend.*

> **clueless when it comes to fashion.**
> *hat keine Ahnung von Mode.*

> **popular with the opposite sex.**
> *beliebt beim anderen Geschlecht.*

a pretty girl.
ein schönes Mädchen.

a handsome guy.
ein attraktiver Kerl.

like a model.
voll Modelmäßig.

looks like a bum.
sieht aus wie ein Penner.

a total nerd.
echt nerdmäßig.

·····Nerding out
Nerdheit

In Germany, nerds aren't really social outcasts, cuz they've got their own friends and they even get laid sometimes. Like a lot of nerds, German ones are just hard-core fired up about whatever they're into. But for some strange reason German nerds are especially into collecting stuff. Sometimes they're overtly proud of their collections and sometimes they hide them like dirty little secrets.

To collect
sammeln

What do you collect?
Was sammelst du?

He's a total...
Er ist ein echter...

> **nerd.**
> *Nerd. (m)*

> **collector nerd.**
> *Sammler-nerd.*

record nerd.
Platten-nerd.

comic book nerd.
Comic-nerd.

computer nerd.
Computer-nerd.

He's/She's kinda nerdy.
*Er/Sie ist etwas **Nerd-mäßig**.*

I'm proud to be a nerd.
Ich bin stolz, Nerd zu sein.

All my best friends are nerds.
Alle meine Kumpels sind Nerds.

Wow, Germans are a bunch of nerds.
*Die Deutschen sind ein echt **Nerd-mäßiges Volk**.*

I just don't get all the nerdiness.
*Diese **Nerdheit** verstehe ich nicht.*

I'm totally into nerds.
Ich bin echt heiß auf Nerds.

COOL, MAN!)))
GEIL, ALDA!

Cool!	*Geil!*
Totally cool!	*Voll geil!*
Insanely cool!	*Mega geil!*
Fuckin' Cool!	*Affengeil!* (literally, "ape horny")
Insanely fuckin' cool!	*Oberaffengeil!*
Totally sick!	*Krass!*
Uncontrollably cool!	*Echt pornös!*

Can I show you my stamp collection?
*Darf ich dir noch meine **Briefmarkensammlung** zeigen?*
'Not only one of the nerdiest things a German can ask you,
it's also a classic, clichéd German pickup line that's really
just an invitation to hop into the sack.

My collection of…is way cooler than yours.
*Meine…**Sammlung** ist viel cooler als deine.*

Ü-eiersammlung
Tons of Germans collect the little toys that come in
Überraschungseier, or little chocolate eggs with a
prize. Some of the toys are worth some serious Euros.
I knew a dude who paid for his year abroad when he
sold his collection.

Telefonkarten
Another huge collectible item is used phone cards.
I shit you not.

Bierdeckel
It seems almost a no-brainer that there's a community
of beer coaster collectors. I've even seen someone
make furniture out of these cardboard wonders.

Hörspiele
Tapes and records of childrens' stories. *TKKG* and *Die
drei Fragezeichen* are childhood classics that are great
to fall asleep to.

·····Comics, cartoons, and cult icons

Comics, Zeichentrickfilme und Kultfiguren

I think the stress of being blamed for two world wars has forced some Germans to escape reality by regressing into the safety of their childhood. They'll surround themselves with kiddy kitsch for comfort. Sometimes it's subtle like a cutesy figurine on their desk or a few comics tucked away by their bed. Other times it's batshit crazy like ladies who wear embroidered denim Looney Tunes shirts, have fifty cats, and only have sex in bunny costumes. In moderation, this fondness for all things childish is cool, but watch out for the crazies.

Comics
Comics (pl)

Asterix und Obelix
Originally a French comic strip, but once they were released in the various German dialects, they achieved cult status. Basically funny stuff happens in a French village of barbarians who've yet to be invaded by the Romans. I don't get it.

Das kleine Arschloch
The Little Asshole
Probably the most popular German comic. The Little Asshole is a nearsighted kid who runs around naked and insults everyone under the sun. The artist Walter Moers is also responsible for *Käpt'n Blaubär* (see below).

Diddl
This horribly annoying, cutesy comic strip mouse is especially popular with girls and lonely women. If someone you meet has anything *Diddl*-related, watch out, you might just get a birthday card with him on it.

EAST GERMAN NOSTALGIA)))
OSTALGIE

Ostalgie is a specific word for nostalgia for all things East German (as in from the former GDR). While some older Germans see it as an inappropriate fixation on an oppressive regime, others are just clinging to the good times they had as kids. Politics aside, it's really just a marketing term to cash in on T-shirts and childhood kitsch with old GDR brands and pop culture figures.

> Aside from the Stasi, the Wall, and the Russians, the GDR wasn't all that bad, was it?
> *Abgesehen von der Stasi, der Mauer, und den Russen, war die DDR nicht so schlimm, oder?*

Cartoons
Zeichentrickfilme (pl)

Kids Shows
Kindersendungen (pl)

Die Sendung mit der Maus
The Show with the Mouse
Like a cross between Saturday morning cartoons and the Discovery Channel for kids. The cartoon mouse, along with his friends the Elephant and the Duck, are German icons and can be found on everything from pajamas and bedsheets to notebooks and coffee mugs.

Löwenzahn
Dandylion
The host Peter Lustig is the German Mr. Rogers, but he lives in a gypsy-like caravan and wears farmer overalls. Despite the immense possibility of creepiness, he's not. Really, he's not.

Die Biene Maja
Maja the Bee
This cartoon from the '70s doesn't get old, at least not if you watched it when you were a kid. She's a cute bee who's always screwing something up and then getting herself out of a jam. Chicks love this show, so play along.

Das Sandmännchen
The Little Sandman
A kids' show hit from the former GDR. The Sandman stars in little stop-motion animation shorts which are shown before kids go to sleep; get it: the Sandman puts them to sleep. He's got friends, too, like *Pittiplatsch*, a weird pygmy elf thing and *Schnatterinchen* the duck.

Käpt'n Blaubär
Capt'n Bluebear
An old Sea Captain, who happens to be a blue bear, tells his grandkids ridiculous stories about his adventures. There's a little double entendre going on with some inside jokes for adults, kinda like *Pee wee's Playhouse* without the public masturbation and felonies.

CHAPTER 8

SPORTY GERMAN
SPORTLICHES DEUTSCH

Despite Germany's cultural and linguistic differences, the one thing that brings them all together is their love of sports. Germans love just about every sport on the planet, but basketball, handball, Formula 1, and cycling are especially high on their list. In a weird twist of Germanic irony, the one sport universally loved by all Germans, *Fußball*, is the very thing that leads to some serious inter-German hatred. At soccer games, German fan loyalty puts your average Yankee fan to shame. Visiting fans arrive at matches more like an invading army than simple rival fans. I once got stuck in a train station where hordes of Schalke 04 fans faced off with fans from Bayern München. I thought I was gonna get trampled to death.

·····Sports
Sport

Do you like to play...
Spielst du gern...

I wanna play…
Ich will…spielen.

Let's watch…
Lass uns…gucken.

>**Ice hockey**
>*Eishockey*

>**Basketball**
>*Basketball*

>**Tennis**
>*Tennis*

>**Hand ball**
>*Handball*
>Olympic hand ball, you know like soccer with your hands. It's pretty popular.

>**Formula 1**
>*Formel eins*

>**American football**
>*Football*

>**Soccer**
>*Fußball* (Hands down the number 1 sport in Germany.)

>**something else**
>*was Anderes*

>**the sports news**
>*die Sportschau* (Germany's equivalent of Sports Center.)

Why are the Germans so crazy about soccer?
Warum sind die Deutschen verrückt nach Fußball?

Which…do you like?
Welche…magst du?

>**Types of sports**
>*Sportarten (pl)*

WEiRD WORLD OF SPORTS)))
AUßERGEWÖHNLICHE SPORTARTEN

The Germans like to drink beer. A lot of it. This might explain why some of the following bizarre sports caught on in Germany.

SO, I'VE NEVER HEARD OF ...
VON ... HABE ICH NIE GEHÖRT.

DO YOU GUYS REALLY PLAY ... ?
SPIELT IHR EIGENTLICH ... ?

Aquaball
It's kinda like a weird combination of soccer and water polo, only you're playing in a kiddy pool and girls mock you.

Autoball
Invented by Stefan Raab (who also introduced the world to Wok-sledding), it's basically demolition derby mixed with soccer.

Klootschießen
"Road bowling" is pretty simple. Find a long stretch of road, a couple of wooden balls, and some bored northern Germans. It's like a combination relay race/shot put. Teams compete for distance by chucking the ball as far as they can, the next teammate starts where the ball lands.

Hakeln
This is Bavarian beer hall tug of war with fingers. Seated across from each other at a massive wooden table, each *Hakler* (roughly translates as "hooker") locks his finger onto a little rope; pull the other guy over the table and you win. Just don't spill your beer.

Teams
Mannschaften (pl)

Players
Spieler (pl)

Jugger

Who else but the Germans would catch on to a weird postapocalyptic game taken from a sci-fi movie? Ok, maybe the Japanese, but then it would have robots and would be super cool. *Jugger*, however, is decidedly uncool. It's like soccer and lacrosse combined with live action role-playing, foam weapons, and a rubber dog's skull for the ball.

Kegeln

This is like tenth-century bowling. You use nine small pins and a small ball without holes. Bowling alleys are catching on in Germany, but the *Kegelbahn* is really where it's at.

Prellball

Kinda like volleyball, except the net is only about 12 inches high and you have to bounce it on your side over the net and hope the other team doesn't send it back. It looks really lame, in case you were wondering.

Rhönradturnen

You know the wheel that clowns roll around in at the circus? It isn't just a stupid trick; it's wheel gymnastics!

Unterwasserrugby

Underwater rugby: yep, exactly what it sounds like.

Schleuderball

Literally, "sling ball." How else can you describe a game where you have to sling a horsehair-filled ball by its handle at the other team's goal?

•••••Bar games
Kneipensport

Bars aren't much more than the last resort to find love or a place to drown your sorrows. Most Germans prefer to get sloshed in a pub-like *Kneipe*, where they can also challenge their friends to useless games of "skill."

Wanna play some…?
Wollen wir mal…?

Do you know how to play…
Kannst du…

…is the shit.
…ist der Hammer.

…isn't really my thing.
…ist nicht mein Ding.

Cards
Karten spielen
Skat is the national card game of Germany. It's like bridge with a smaller deck and is more confusing if you're drunk. I think only old people really get it.

Dice
knobeln
Kinda like Yahtzee, but less nerdy and more trash talk. People play this for hours, usually for drinks.

Pool
Billiard spielen

Ping-pong
Tischtennis spielen

Darts
Dart spielen

Pinball
flippern

Bowling
bowlen

Foosball
kickern
This is huge in almost every *Kneipe*. Foosball gets its name from *Fußball*. If you think you're good at it just because you can beat everyone in your dorm, wait until you play the Germans. They're demons at *Kickern*.

Table soccer
Tipp-Kick spielen
Not foosball, but a hugely popular and a kinda dorky/
kinda cool game where two dudes face off on a felt
field with two little soccer player figures. Basically
you just push the button on your player's head and
he kicks a black and white octagonal ball at a little
goal. They've even got national *Tipp-Kick spielen*
tournaments for serious nerds.

•••••Outdoor recreation
Freiluftsport

Germans are totally into the outdoors. Any chance they have
to get in tune with nature, they jump at it, especially if they
can do it in the nude. For whatever reason, Germans just love
being outside and naked.

Wanna go...?
Wollen wir...?

sun bathing
sonnenbaden

to the nude beach
zum FKK Strand
FKK stands for *Freikörperkultur* or "free body culture" and it
ain't all that sexy.

hiking
wandern

wakeboarding
wakeboarden

mountain biking
Mountainbike fahren

rock climbing
klettern

kayaking
Kajak fahren

canoeing
paddeln

on a bike tour
eine Radtour machen

camping
zelten
Camping in Germany is kind of a pain. You can't camp
in the wild, so lots of people spend the summers at
official campsites on the beaches in the north, in the
Alps, or at some lakes. If you're feeling adventurous,
plenty of farmers are willing to let you stay on their land
as long as you clean up after yourself, so make sure
you take your empties with you.

to an open festival
zum Open-air gehen
Kinda like camping, only with 20,000 punkers, emos
and metal kids.

·····The national team
die Mannschaft

The European Championships and the World Cup are the few
times that die-hard *Fußball* rivals get behind the one team that
they can all cheer for: the German national team.

Which team has the kickoff?
*Welche Mannschaft hat **Anstoß**?*

That header was awesome!
***Der Kopfstoß** war echt der Hammer!*

He's getting the ass card! (red card)
*Der hat **die Arschkarte gezogen**!*
Since the ref pulls the red card out of his back pocket, it's
called "drawing the ass card." The phrase can be used in
soccer or to describe any situation where you're shit out
of luck.

Was that a bicycle kick?
War das 'n Scherenschlag?

He's afraid of the penalty kick!
*Er hat Schiss vorm **Elfer**!*

So where are all the hooligans?
*Wo sind denn die ganzen **Hooligans**?*
German hooligans are mostly right-wing skins who hang around looking pissed, complaining about Poland. The riot cops show up at train stations and stadiums on game days to help keep the peace, but seeing them decked out with their tactical shields and helmets can scare the shit out of newbies.

Dude, I really need get hooked up with the club colors!
*Alda, ich brauche doch 'ne coole **Kutte**!*
German soccer fans can kinda be like bikers. They drink a lot, get rowdy, and they wear their own colors. The *Kutte* is like a sleeveless jean jacket covered with about 50 patches from your favorite team on it. You'll probably find some dried blood or vomit on it, too.

Check out all the cute little ball-boys.
*Schau mal, die süßen **Auflaufkinder**. (pl)*
These are the kids from the kiddy leagues who run out with the pro players on the field before matches. They're sort of like the team's mascot, but their only job is to stand there. The term literally means "kids that run out" and they're fun to make fun of.

Schal (m)

Like the *Kutte*, the team scarf is like a fan's version of a security blanket. They bring it with them to every game, wear it even when it's not cold, and swing it at matches to get all fired up.

> **Aren't scarves kinda lame?**
> *Sind die **Schals** nicht etwas uncool?*

> **I'd rather watch the game at the Fan-zone.**
> *Das Spiel würde ich lieber in der **Fan-zone** gucken.*
> These are the massive outdoor viewing areas set up for the World Cup and European Championships. It's basically a giant tailgate party with better food and beer, plus you actually get to watch the match.

SOME PEARLS OF SOCCER WISDOM

> **"The ball is round and a match lasts 90 minutes."**
> *"Der Ball ist rund und ein Spiel dauert 90 Minuten."*
> This is a famous motivational quote from Sepp Herberger, the coach of Germany's 1954 World Cup championship team. Herberger, philosophical genius that he was, also gave us these gems:

>> **"The round thing has to go in the square thing."**
>> *"Das Runde muss in das Eckige."*

>> **"Sometimes you lose, sometimes the other guy wins."**
>> *"Mal verliert man, mal gewinnen die Anderen."*

>> **"After the game is before the game."**
>> *"Nach dem Spiel ist vor dem Spiel."*

> National hero, that Sepp.

·····Cheering
Jubeln

German sports fans are totally fanatic, you might even say freakishly territorial, about their home teams. It all comes down to their hard-core regional identity as Berliners, Hamburgers,

Bremers, Dresdners, etc. Rooting for anyone but the home team is the social equivalent of pissing in someone else's pool, and you're likely to get shunned at an early age for it.

Hurray!
Hurrah!

Goooooo!
Looooos!

Shoot!
Schieß los!

Gooooooal!
Tooooor!

The ref is fuckin' nuts!
Der Schiri hat 'ne Macke!

Aw, come on!
Na, komm schon!

The goalie's got a clubbed foot!
Der Schlussmann hat 'nen Klumpfuß!

Fuckin' Munich fans.
Scheiß München Fans.

Murder 'em!
Bringt sie um!

How can I get season tickets?
Wie kriege ich eine Dauerkarte?

Can you help me out with the rules?
Kannste' mir mal die Spielregeln erklären?

Are you a **hard-core fan?**
*Bist du ein **hardcore Freak**?*

Are you FC St. Pauli **supporters?**
*Seid ihr FC St. Pauli **Retter**?*
Hamburg's FC St. Pauli is Germany's only punk-approved
soccer club. St. Pauli is famous for its punks, the
Reeperbahn and its red-light district. In danger of going
under due to lack of sponsors, *Retter*, or literally "saviors,"
stepped in by buying tons of merch and drumming up
interest and sponsors for the club. Fuck Bayern München;
FC St. Pauli for life!

Do you know any cool **chants?**
*Kennste coole **Chants**?*

·····Chants
Fangesänge

Germans don't have marching bands, so they gotta sing to
get themselves fired up at sporting events. There's something
beautiful about 20,000 *Fußball* fans telling each other and
their respective teams to get bent. Each team has its own
chants that go in and out of style, but some die-hard favorites
include:

TO THE OTHER TEAM
(sung to the tune of "When the Saints Go Marching In")

Ihr habt bezahlt, ihr könnt jetzt gehen…(3x)
You paid your dough, it's time to go…(3x)

(or this classic, which is really just a taunt)

Ihr könnt nach Hause geh'n
Ihr könnt nach Hause geh'n
Ihr könnt nach Haus, Ihr könnt nach Hause geh'n.
You can all go home,
You can all go home,
You can all, You can all go home right now.

FOR YOUR TEAM

(another classic taunt)

Einer geht noch, einer geht noch rein,
Einer geht noch, einer geht noch rein.
Time to score one, time to score one more,
Time to score one, time to score one more.

(sung to the tune of "Oh My Darling, Clementine")

Immer wieder, immer wieder,
immer wieder (insert name of favorite team)**,**
von der Elbe bis zur Isar,
immer wieder (insert name of favorite team)*!*
Now and always, now and always,
Now and always (insert name of favorite team)
From the Elbe to the Isar*
Now and always (insert name of favorite team)!

*The Isar and Elbe are two German rivers that mark off boundaries from north to south.

The following song was written by *Fußball* legend Franz Beckenbauer while on the national team in 1966 and has become a cult classic. Learn it and you'll score some new pals.

Gute Freunde kann niemand trennen,
gute Freunde sind nie allein.
Weil sie eines im Leben können,
füreinander da zu sein.
No one can split up good friends,
Good friends are never alone.
'Cuz in life they're only able,
to be there in the end.

·····Exercise
Training

In general, Germans are pretty health conscious and try to stay active. Going to the gym isn't as big as it is in the States, but most people join some sort of sports club or *Sportverein* where they really get into whatever sport that twists their pretzel. Of course, it's not just exercise or training, but a way to hang out and even go out for a beer or two afterwards.

Hey, you guys know where I can…?
Hey, wisst ihr, wo ich…kann?

exercise
trainieren

do some sports
Sport treiben

box
boxen

find a gym
ein Fitness Studio finden

find a sporting club
einen Sportverein finden

lift some weights
Gewichte heben

go swimming
schwimmen

go jogging
joggen gehen

do some circuit training
Circuittraining machen

I should do some more…
Ich sollte mehr…

warm-ups.
aufwärmen.

sit-ups.
Aufrichter machen.

push-ups.
Liegestützen machen.

pull-ups.
Klimmzüge machen.

squats.
Kniebeugen machen.

Should I work my…?
Sollte ich an meine…arbeiten?

> **biceps**
> *Bizeps*
>
> **triceps**
> *Trizeps*
>
> **pecs**
> *Brustmuskel*
>
> **thighs**
> *Oberschenkel*
>
> **calves**
> *Waden*
>
> **ass**
> *Pomuskeln* (your butt muscles)
>
> **gut**
> *Bauchmuskeln*

Should we go for a run?
Sollten wir laufen gehen?

I'm not a big fan of the gym!
*Ich bin kein großer Fan von **Muckibuden**!*
The "*Muckibude*" is literally the muscle shack.

I'm totally sore.
Ich habe voll die Muskelkater.

I'm sweating like a pig!
Ich schwitze wie Sau!

I'm totally outta breath!
Ich bin voll außer Atem!

I guess I could use some practice.
Ich sollte vielleicht doch ein bisschen üben.

CHAPTER 9

HUNGRY GERMAN
HUNGRIGES DEUTSCH

•••••Hunger
Hunger (m)

When Germans get the munchies, they take ownership of their growling guts by describing being hungry as actually "having hunger" (*Hunger haben*). Letting everyone know just how hungry you are can be just as important as the food you eat to quiet the monster in your belly, so express your need to feed accordingly with the following morsels.

I'm...
Ich...

a little hungry.
habe nur ein bisschen Hunger.

hungry.
habe Hunger.

not hungry at all.
habe keinen Hunger.

famished.
habe Schmacht.

starving Marvin!
habe tierischen Kohldampf!

starting to digest myself.
verdaure mich gerade selbst.

stuffed.
bin satt.

thirsty.
habe Durst.

parched.
habe einen Brand.

dying of thirst here.
habe voll den Mordsbrand.

I'm so hungry I could eat a horse.
Mein Magen hängt in den Kniekehlen.
Literally, "my stomach is hanging at my kneecaps"

My belly...
Mein Magen...

> **is empty.**
> *ist leer.*
>
> **is full.**
> *ist voll.*
>
> **is gonna burst.**
> *platzt gleich.*
>
> **is killing me.**
> *tut mir weh.*
>
> **is grumbling.**
> *knurrt.*

·····Food
Essen (n)

Food is awesome. If you don't eat it, you die. Need I say more? Germans take eating pretty seriously. It's so important to them that they've got multiple words for it, be it *Lebensmittel* (the means of life), *Nahrungsmittel* (the means of nourishment), or simply *Essen* (food). Whether you're cooking at home, going out to grab a *Dönerkebab,* or just chilling and ordering a pizza, use these essentials to get by.

You eat yet?
Haste schon gegessen?

Wanna grab a bite?
Wollen wir was ins Gesicht schieben?
Literally, "wanna shove something in your face?"

I gotta eat something.
Ich muss was essen.

Let's pig out!
Lass uns fressen!

What do you like to eat?
Was isst du gern?

Is there a health food store around here?
Gibt's irgendwo in der Nähe ein Reformhaus?

What's your favorite food?
Was it dein Lieblingsessen?

Should I cook you up something?
Sollte ich dir was kochen?

Let's go out to eat.
Lass uns essen gehen.

Maybe we should call for take out.
Vielleicht sollten wir den Lieferservice anrufen.

You wanna just order a pizza?
Willste einfach 'ne Pizza bestellen?

You can't get good pretzels anywhere in the U.S.
In den Staaten kriegt man keine vernünftigen Brezeln.

I don't really like…food.
…Essen mag ich nicht so sehr.

Dude, I'm jonesing for something…
Ich hab' voll Bock auf was…

> **greasy.**
> *fettiges.*
>
> **healthy.**
> *gesundes.*
>
> **tasty.**
> *leckeres.*
>
> **exotic.**
> *exotisches.*
>
> **Greek.**
> *griechisches.*
>
> **Turkish.**
> *türkisches.*
>
> **German.**
> *deutsches.*
>
> **fancy.**
> *feines.*
>
> **vegetarian.**
> *vegetarisches.*
>
> **quick.**
> *schnelles.*
>
> **huge.**
> *großes.*

·····Eating out
Essen gehen

Most Germans like to cook at home rather than eat out. I had
to convince a German roommate once that ordering a pizza

didn't make me lazy, just hungry for pizza. When Germans go out to dinner, it's usually part of a night out, like before hitting the clubs or when going out on a date. There aren't a lot of chain restaurants in Germany besides American fast food places, which are just as shitty there as they are at home. But why waste your time on American fast food anyway? Every major German city has tons of great international restaurants to choose from, and Germans are always more than happy to recommend their favorite organic-raw-vegan Thai joint or whatever.

When deciding on a cuisine, instead of saying, "Let's go to an Italian restaurant," for example, slang it up by saying "*Lass uns zum Italiener*" ("Let's go to the Italians"), which is basically like saying "Let's grab some Italian" in English.

Let's grab some…
Lass uns zum…

Italian food.
Italiener.
Fuck the Olive Garden. Italian food in Germany is legit and is the closest to the real thing you'll find without getting run over by some dick on a Vespa in Rome.

Mexican food.
Mexikaner.
I'm from Southern California and love Mexican food. Mexican food in Germany is almost nonexistent and when you can find it, it usually makes Taco Bell look gourmet. I did find some good tacos in Berlin and a tasty burrito in Essen, but that was the exception, not the rule.

Indian food.
Inder.
Indian food is always great, but for some reason it's especially amazing in Germany. Don't ask why, it just is. The menus are usually a weird mixture of English and German, which hilariously leads to descriptions like "hot dick curry."

Japanese food.
Japaner.
Is it just me or are most Japanese restaurants in America run by Koreans or Chinese? This seems to be the case for most sushi places in Germany, too.

Chinese food.
Chinesen.
I like Chinese food alright, but it's not really all that different in Germany than it is in the States, except maybe less greasy. There are a lot of Chinese restaurants in the Fatherland, but they always seem empty and kinda sad to me.

Vietnamese food.
Vietnamesen.
East Germany had lots of guest workers from Vietnam who stayed after the Berlin Wall fell, and it seems like they all opened restaurants. Most of the ones I've seen seem like a weird combination of Vietnamese and Chinese fast food, but there are some really good soup shops, too.

Turkish food.
Türken.
Turkish food is like the Mexican food of Germany. It's tasty, cheap and there's a Turkish joint on nearly every corner. They're especially prevalent in the north, and the Kreuzberg district in Berlin is the German birthplace of the delicious *Dönerkebab*.

Greek food.
Griechen.
Greek food rules. It's really similar to and almost as popular as Turkish food, but don't confuse the two or they might spit in your gyro.

Persian food.
Perser.
Lots of Persian restaraunts will describe themselves as *Orientalisch* or "from the Orient." For those who failed your course on ancient civilization, it means Persia, not Asia. The food is insanely good and amazingly colorful and diverse. If you're a vegetarian, you're set cuz there are tons of veggie dishes to choose from.

·····The snack shop
Imbiss (m)

These small snack shops (*Imbiss* means "snack") are the German equivalents of taco trucks and roach coaches. They're the number one place where everyone from businessmen to punkers rub elbows and eat some really good street food on the cheap. Lots of legit restaurants also operate an *Imbiss* for people who want to eat on the run or while staggering home from a club. One of the most important things to remember is that *Imbiss*-slang (*Imbiss-deutsch*) is hard-core street slang… the closest thing to scumbag German (*Asi-deutsch*) without actually being a scumbag. There are four golden rules:

1. Be brief when ordering. Hungry drunk people don't want to waste their time with extra words and syllables.

Fries with catsup.
Einmal Pommes mit Ketchup.

2. Don't use articles. This is the one time you really don't need to use der/die/das, but if you do use an article, make sure it is *den*, the *Imbiss* article of choice regardless of gender or quantity.

The order of fries!
Den Pommes!

3. When you go to pick up your food, you don't say, "I ordered the sausage." You say, "I *am* the sausage."

I'm the sausage.
Ich bin den Wurst.

4. Never use plurals. If you want to order two or more of something, just use the number and the singular form of the noun.

Two Bratwurst.
Zweimal Bratwurst.

Gimme a...
Einmal...

Döner. (m)
Dönerkebab is the Turkish version of a gyro. Walk
by almost any Turkish *Imbiss* and you'll see what
looks like a giant cone of meat (usually lamb, beef, or
sometimes chicken) spinning on a spit in an upright
rotisserie. Stand mesmerized as the grill master slices
off strips of the meat with a giant knife into an awaiting
pita or *Fladenbrot* (Turkish flatbread) before being
garnished with pickled cabbage and a garlic-yogurt
tzatziki sauce. This is absolutely the best thing before,
during, or after a night of hard partying.

Döner **makes you prettier!**
Döner **macht Schöner!**
As if the idea of bread stuffed with meat from a spit
isn't attractive enough, the *Döner* industry came up
with this amazing slogan. It comes in handy when your
friends ask why you are eating like five of them in a
sitting.

Pommes. (pl)
German French fries make fries from Mickey D's or BK
taste like Mr. Potato Head's fried poop.

Pommes are thick cut, double fried (yup, double fried),
and come with any kind of sauce imaginable. *Pommes
rot/weiß* or *Pommes Schranke* gets you mayonnaise,
catsup, and probably a mean case of diarrhea.

Frikadelle. (f)
Sometimes called *Bulette*, *Klopse*, *Frika,* or *Grilletta*,
this is the granddaddy of the American hamburger.
Frikadellen look a little like football-shaped
hamburgers. The meat's got garlic, onion, and a few
other spices in it, and is far superior to just about
anything you call a burger. Eat one in the morning with
a roll and mustard and you'll forget that you were ever
hungover.

THE BEST OF THE WURST)))
DAS BESTE VON DER WURST

Because Germans don't dick around when it comes to sausage ...

Presskopf (m)
Did you know that head cheese is really a kind of sausage? It's really kind of gross, too.

Zungenwurst (f)
Like head cheese, but made from cows' tongues instead of the meat around the head.

Blutwurst (f)
Blood sausage is, well, sausage made from cooked blood, grains, and some pig fat. It tastes like a rusty nail.

Knackwurst (f)
Named after the cracking sound they make when you bite into the intestinal casing. Their contents vary from region to region.

Leberwurst (f)
This is straight up liver sausage, but don't think of calling it liverwurst. It's a fantastic concoction of liver, spices, pork, and other innards.

Teewurst (f)
No one really knows why it's called "tea sausage" but with 40 percent fat, it's basically meat butter.

Wattwurm (f)
From *Ostfriesland* in the northwest, these "mud worms" are like smokier, saltier, foot-and-a-half long Slim Jims. They're great with beer. Think of them as meat pretzels.

Bratwurst (f)
Any grilled sausage, usually, but not always (see below), pork or beef.

Ross-bratwurst (f)
Horse: the other bratwurst meat. I'm not sure how you feel about eating Mr. Ed, but these are rare and immensely tasty treats. Get them at the *Freimarkt* in Bremen. *Danke* Timm!

Thüringer (m)
Made with garlic and spices, these flavorful favorites from the southeast are the king of the *Bratwürste*.

Lahmacun. (f)
Turkish pizza isn't really pizza, but thin Turkish bread with spices and sauce. But it's close enough. Try one rolled up with *Dönerkebab* meat in it. You'll thank me many times.

Currywurst. (f)
Also referred to as just a *C-wurst*. The Hamburg-Berlin rivalry is brutal when it comes to who makes the best of these sliced up sausages doused in catsup and curry powder. A *C-wurst* is the next best thing to *Döner* for your drunken crawls home. If you're ever in the St. Pauli district in Hamburg be sure to hit up the *Imbiss bei Schorsch* for one of these. They're the king of the *C-wurst*.

Bockwurst. (f)
Also called *B-wurst*, these are like those foot-long dogs from the ballpark, only they don't suck or cost twelve bucks. You don't eat *B-wurst* with the traditional bun, though. Instead, you eat them with a slice of bread and lots of mustard.

Brötchen. (n)
These little rolls are a German staple. No matter how hungover your friends are, at least one will crawl down to the baker and buy a bag of these so everyone can eat breakfast. Butter them up, throw on some jam or cheese and meat, and you're golden.

Schnitzel. (n)
Thin, breaded, fried meat, usually veal or pork, but can also be chicken, turkey, or even tofu for you animal-friendly types. Squeeze a lemon over it and wolf it

down with a plate of fries and a nice cold beer…or just ask for a *Schnipopi*, short for *Schnitzel, Pommes und Pils* (Schnitzel, fries, and a beer).

·····Fast food
Fastfood (n)

Germans have a love-hate relationship with fast food. The socially conscious part of them despises the idea of chains and the lack of nutritional value, but the lazy, antisocial, hungover side of them craves the *McDrive*. If they do eat at a fast food joint, they do so begrudgingly, making fun of it at the same time. And their regional pride usually kicks in, too, making them choose a locally owned fast food joint rather than a larger international chain. These German fast food outlets are supposedly healthier than their international (i.e., U.S.) counterparts, something the health-conscious Krauts dig. That being said, you can still get your grease on at any of the following.

Do you really want to eat at…?
Willste wirklich bei….essen?

I can't eat at…anymore.
Ich kann nie wieder bei…essen.

…is worse than eating out of a trash can.
…ist schlimmer als aus der Mülltonne zu essen.

…ain't all that bad.
…ist gar nicht so schlecht.

…gives me the shits.
Ich kriege immer Flitzekacke von…

Nordsee
Where else can you get a cold fish sandwich (*Fischbrötchen*)? Okay, in Germany you can get those

almost anywhere, but *Nordsee* shreds and I don't even like fish.

Wienerwald

This is a fast food chicken joint from Austria whose name means "the Viennese forest." Sure it sounds pretty magical, but it's really just a Euro version of KFC. At least the chicken here is roasted instead of fried and doesn't taste like a greasy sponge.

Kochlöffel

The "Cooking Spoon" is a truly German fast food chain that's been around since the '60s. They do chicken and burgers and are the only place I know of in Germany where you can get those weird fried meat croquets you find in Dutch vending machines. Those things look like fried cat turds, but taste delicious, even when you're sober.

McDonald's

Germans call it *McDoof* (McStupid) but on occasion they'll still eat here. The drive-thru is called *McDrive* and every one of them serves beer.

Burger King

Lovingly referred to as *Würger Schling* (the hangman's noose).

Kentucky Fried Chicken

Everyone in Germany calls KFC "Kentucky *schreit ficken*" because it rhymes with "Kentucky Fried Chicken" but means "Kentucky scream fuck." Apparently, this is funny to Germans. In addition to mediocre fried chicken, KFC serves donuts and chili cheese fries too.

Pizza Hut

Their slogan is "The American Way of Pizza." It's about as "good" as it is in the States, but the one near my house had an all-you-can-eat-pizza night with free soda refills. Since no German restaurants—fast food or otherwise—offer free refills, this is like finding money in the street.

·····Cafés
Cafes

American-style coffee chains are kinda new here and the serious coffee-drinking Germans have taken a while to warm up to them. The Germans are an enviro-conscious bunch and cringe a bit at the thought of all those paper cups, plastic lids, and the "coffee to go" culture that flies in the face of their idea of coffee as a leisure activity. Nevertheless "American-style" coffee houses have popped up. But unsurprisingly in mega-corporation-hating Germany, smaller chains tend to do far better than that global coffee monolith from Seattle.

Tchibo
They pioneered the term "coffee to go" and have got coffee shops, a travel agency, and mail order catalog all in one shop. If you got a crappy gift from some German aunt, it probably came from Tchibo.

Balzac Coffee
It's pretty much the German version of Starbucks. You can even get tea here with those weird tapioca balls.

Starbucks
The corporate coffee concept is so foreign to Germans that Starbucks had to come up with a worksheet to help customers order using their annoying brand of barrista-speak.

Woytons
This is a smaller chain that serves your usual café assortment of soup, salads, sandwiches, and snacks. The fact that they're a smaller chain makes them cool, but it also helps that they don't play weak-sauce pussy rock (i.e., Dave Matthews Band) on the sound system.

Bagel Brothers
This is really the only place to go for bagels because, well, it's really the only place in Germany that makes bagels. That's not a bad thing, though, cuz the bagels here are pretty kick-ass.

Ditsch
Not really a coffee shop, but I wanted to give them some cred because of the wonders they work with pretzels.

Seriously, it's scary how good these things are. If you're a fan of pizza-bagels, you'll freak out over the *Tomaten-Käse Stange*; a pretzel-pizza roll that tastes like nothing you've ever had before. I ate six of these in one sitting once and felt like a pretzel god.

LeCrobag

Peddlers of coffee and "French-style" pastries, which consist mostly of croissants filled with anything imaginable. The marzipan ones are the best, even if you're not a twelve-year-old kid. Like *Ditsch*, you'll find a *LeCrobag* at nearly every subway or train station.

·····Yummmmy!
Lecker!

Medieval Germans used to burp and fart their asses off at the table as a sign of satisfaction and gratitude. Luckily, we've emerged from the Dark Ages and you no longer have to thank your host by airing out your large intestine. These days, if you really want to show that you're enjoying yourself, let everyone know with some of these.

Tasty!
Lecker!

Yummilicious!
Schmackofatzig!

Hmmm, tasty tasty!
Hmmm, legga legga!

That was amazing.
Das war aber herrlich.

You're totally mowing that down.
Das haste voll aufgezehrt.

Wow, you can really wolf it down!
Mannomann, kannst du was wegschaufeln!

Awesome, totally awesome.
Fabelhaft, einfach fabelhaft.

The cook's a total genius.
Der Koch ist ein Genie.

Man o manischewitz, this is the shit!
Heidewitzka, ist das aber legga!

Can I get seconds?
Gibt's 'nen Nachschlag?

That's smells incredible.
Das riecht aber wunderbar.

·····Yuck!
Bäähh!

You know that bald guy on TV who travels the world eating bull balls and pig brains? On German TV he's called *Der Alles-Esser*, or "the guy who eats everything." He eats tons of nasty shit, but never gets grossed out. Impress your friends by showing your disgust the next time you see him chowing down on monkey rectum.

Disgusting!
Widerlich!

That's like totally icky.
Das ist aber voll ekelig.

That's gross!
Pfui!

That's really gross!
Pfui extra!

That's really fucking gross!
Pfui extra gold!

This looks like a shitheap.
*Das sieht aus wie ein **Misthaufen**.*

I don't like how...
tastes.
...schmeckt mir nicht.

...tastes nasty.
*...schmeckt aber **ekelhaft**.*

...tastes like shit.
*...schmeckt **wie Scheiße**.*

...smells like baby poo.
*...riecht **wie Baby A-A**.* (pronounced like "ah-ah")

...smells like the morgue.
*...stink **wie die Leichenhalle**.*

> **Sauerkraut**
> *Sauerkraut*
>
> **Cauliflower**
> *Blumenkohl*
>
> **Liverwurst**
> *Leberwurst*
>
> **Swiss cheese**
> *Emmentaler*

What's that smell?
*Was ist das für ein **Gestank**?*

WEiRD GERMAN SPECiALTiES)))

Germans don't eat many weird animals like in Asia or Africa, but they do have some insane dishes made from parts that "normal" people throw out.

NORTH GERMAN SPECIALTIES

Bremer Kükenragout
This "baby chicken stew" is a rare delicacy that both intrigues and disgusts at the same time. It's made with young chickens, shrimp, crawfish tails, and beef tongue. Yumm!

Grünkohl und Pinkel
Northern German soul food. *Grünkohl* isn't cabbage at all, but steamed kale cooked with super salty bacon that you eat with a special sausage called *Pinkel*. *Pinkel* actually gets its name from the verb to piss, or *pinkeln*, since when sausages get cooked they drip from the tip as if pissing. In the northwest, where this originates, groups organize a *Kohlfahrt*, or "Kohl-trip" where everyone piles into a bus, gets incredibly drunk, and pigs out on this dish.

Schwarzsauer
This blood soup originated in eastern Prussia, but still delights and terrifies northern Germans to this day. Essentially pig's blood, vinegar, some leftover meat scraps, and pork fat. The vinegar turns the blood black (*Schwarz*) and is sour (*sauer*), hence the incredibly creative name.

Eisbein
A Berlin tradition, *Eisbein* is boiled "pig knuckle" or pork hock (everywhere else in Germany it comes roasted) so it stays juicy and you can pull it off the bone. It's served on a bed of sauerkraut and with tons of beer. It looks gruesome, but is a pork lover's dream.

Moppelkotze
What can you say about a stew that is lovingly referred to as "puppy puke"? Not much, other than that's how some northern Germans refer to an *Eintopf* or "one-pot." There's no set recipe to an *Eintopf*; you just throw whatever stew-friendly ingredients you have around into a pot and let it stew. I guess the end result does look kinda pukey.

CENTRAL GERMAN SPECIALTIES

Saumagen
Another creatively titled dish. Sow's stomach is pretty much the German version of a Scottish haggis, only all the ingredients (vegetables, pork, spices, and potatoes) are stuffed into a pig's stomach and cooked. You eat the stuffing and leave the stomach.

Handkäse mit Musik
Traditional pub-grub from the central German state of Hessen. This "hand-cheese with music" is a kind of waxy cheese that's served with an herb dressing and sliced onions. The name comes from the fact that if you eat a lot of cheese and onions you're probably gonna make ass music all night. Most Kneipen owners offer a version "without music" too as a courtesy to the other guests. But if you're gonna try it just once, you might as well go for the real deal. Remember to wash it down with lots of hard German cider and you'll fit right in.

Sauerbraten
This "sour roast" is traditionally made from horse meat, though today it's more often beef, marinated in a vinegar spice mixture before roasting. Eat it with Rotkohl, the red cabbage cousin to Sauerkraut.

SOUTH GERMAN SPECIALTIES

Hasenpfeffer
A Black Forest specialty consisting of all the shitty, leftover parts of a rabbit cooked in a peppery stew. You can also get the same thing with pork (Schweinepfeffer) or goose (Gänsepfeffer) if eating Bugs Bunny bums you out.

Flädlesuppe
This is basically pancake soup, and yes, it's as weird as it sounds. If you end up in Baden Württemberg make sure you at least get a look at this. It's beef broth served with coils of crepe-like pancakes in it.

Leberkäse
A sort of sausage loaf that looks like a square of bologna and comes served with either an egg (sunny-side up) and mashed potatoes, or warm with a roll and mustard. The markets in Munich sell this stuff like crazy. Try it if you're starving or like eating giant meat-flavored erasers.

That shit reeks.
Das riecht aber übel.

No thanks, I don't eat poop.
Nee, Kacke esse ich nicht.

I can't eat this.
Sowas kann ich nicht essen.

You really gonna eat that shit?
Willst du den Scheiß wirklich essen?

This place is really crappy.
Die Bude hier ist das Allerletzte.

Call an ambulance, I'm gonna be sick!
Ruf den Notarzt, mir wird's schlecht!

Let's bail.
Lass uns abhauen.

⋯⋯Check please!
Die Rechnung bitte!

The food at most *Kneipen*, *Gaststätten,* and *Lokale* is usually pretty good, but the wait staff can often be crappy. It's not unusual to find yourself waiting around for your bill while your waiter disappears for a smoke or even a beer. Lousy service is the result of a culture that prefers to leave diners alone to enjoy their meal, rather than bug them. It doesn't help that tax and tip are technically included in the cost of your meal, giving waiters little incentive to go the extra mile. Additional tipping is becoming much more expected these days, however. Though it's not yet on par with the 15–20 percent you're expected to leave in the States, it's now customary to leave 10 percent.

Pardon me...
Entschuldigung...

> **can I see the menu?**
> *kann ich **die Karte** sehen?*

> **got any specials?**
> *gibt's ein **Tagesmenü**?*

> **what do you recommend?**
> *was **empfehlen** Sie?*

> **is there meat in that?**
> *gibt's **Fleisch drin**?*

Is that organic?
*Ist das **Bio**?*

How big are the portions?
*Wie groß sind **die Portionen**?*

We'd like to order.
*Wir möchten gerne **bestellen**.*

Can I get a knife?
*Kann ich auch **ein Messer** haben?*

Can I get that without...?
*Kriege ich das auch **ohne**...?*

> **tomatoes**
> *Tomaten*

> **mushrooms**
> *Champignons*

> **bacon**
> *Speck*

> **cheese**
> *Käse*

I didn't order this crap.
***Diesen Dreck** habe ich nicht bestellt.*

Do you have dessert too?
Gibt's auch Nachtisch?

This looks a little weird.
Das hier sieht komisch aus.

We're in kind of a hurry.
Wir habn's aber etwas eilig.

We wanna pay.
Wir wollen zahlen.

Can you wrap that up to go?
Können Sie das einpacken?

When's your shift end?
Wann haste Feierabend?

·····Other Ulysses Press Titles

Dirty French: Everyday Slang from "What's Up?" to "F*%# Off!"
ADRIEN CLAUTRIER & HENRY ROWE, **$10.00**

There are enough insults and swear words in this book to offend every person in France without even speaking to them in English.

Dirty Spanish: Everyday Slang from "What's Up?" to "F*%# Off!"
JUAN CABALLERO & NICK DENTON-BROWN, **$10.00**

This handbook, featuring slang for both Spain and Latin America, includes a section on native banter that will help readers convince the local taco maker that it's OK to spice things up with a few fresh habaneros.

Dirty Japanese: Everyday Slang from "What's Up?" to "F*%# Off!"
MATT FARGO, **$10.00**

This book fills in the gap between how people really talk in Japan and what Japanese language students are taught.

Dirty Russian: Everyday Slang from "What's Up?" to "F*%# Off!"
ERIN COYNE & IGOR FISUN, **$10.00**

An invaluable guide for anyone going to Russia, this book is packed with enough insults and swear words to offend every person in Russia without even mentioning that they lost the Cold War.

To order these books call 800-377-2542 or 510-601-8301, fax 510-601-8307, e-mail ulysses@ulyssespress.com, or write to Ulysses Press, P.O. Box 3440, Berkeley, CA 94703. All retail orders are shipped free of charge. California residents must include sales tax. Allow two to three weeks for delivery.

·····About the Author

Daniel Chaffey is a writer, scholar, educator and eternal student of all things German. He has lived and worked in Germany for much of the last 12 years as a student, Fulbright Teaching Associate, translator and bartender, where he perfected his high German skills and learned to converse like a German sailor. He holds an MA in German Studies and a teaching credential from Cal State Long Beach. He currently teaches German in Northern California where he continues to work on other projects, including a lexicon of soldier slang from the Second World War. Visit his website at www.dirtygermanbook.com.